# The Oak Island Connection
## to
# North Africa
## and
# The Illinois Caves Discovery

© 2021 Jack MacNab

Edited and Arranged by Hammerson Peters

# The Oak Island Connection to North Africa and the Illinois Caves Discovery

# By Jack MacNab

# Table of Contents

Introduction……………………………………………..5

Cleopatra Hieroglyphs……………………………………...7

1: Oak Island HO-Stone and the 90-foot Inscribed Stone……10

2: The Queen Scotia Update…………………………………19

3: The Marion County Illinois Caves Discovery…………...28

4: The Marion County Illinois Caves Explained…………...31

5: Glooscap and his Younger Brother Malsum……………….40

6. Oak Island and the Temple of Umglebemu………………...45

7. History of Oak Island Nova Scotia Post-1795…………...50

8. The Norse discoveries of North America ……………….62

9. The 1399 Zeno Voyage to Newfoundland………….............84

10. The Atlantis 2-Second Clock……………………….....98

11. Oak Island and the Azimuth Lines……………….......105

# Introduction

The purpose of this book is to review *two-caves* that are located in North America that need to be investigated! These *two-caves* have also been referred to as *chambers* and *tombs* that may have contained treasures of great historical value, inscribed stones, sarcophagus, etc.

One *cave* is located on Oak Island Nova Scotia Canada! This small island has been an ongoing treasure hunt for more than 200 years. To this very day it is believed by many, that there is a cave-like-chamber located at least 235-feet underground in what is known as the famous Oak Island Money Pit.

A second *cave* is located in Marion County Illinois USA! There is a cave-like-chamber located in a *ravine* area in that county, that has been claimed to have been entered by more than one person over the years. There has been an ongoing quest to locate that *cave* portal for the past 95 years. Yet, to this very day that *cave* continues to elude many treasure searchers.

This book is being presented as investigative historical research project on my part. It is believed by many that the Oak Island Money Pit, and the Illinois Cave are to be viewed only a hoax. That is one motivating force that inspires me to publish this book! This is a quest that I feel needs solid answers. Will I find those answers? Time will tell.

This book also includes various other discoveries that I have made over the years. Plus, the Norsemen coming to North America a 1000 years ago and the 1399 A.D., Zeno voyage to Newfoundland and much more. Hope you find this read to be very interesting. This book should be viewed as continuation of my most recently published book: "Queen Scotia and the Egyptian Connection to Oak Island."

# Cleopatra Hieroglyphs, Admiral's Cove, Bedford Basin Nova Scotia

In and about 1988-99, I discovered five hieroglyphs in the Admiral's Cove area of Bedford Basin Nova Scotia. For the longest time, I had concluded that they were possibly carved on that stone surface by Egyptians who may have made a voyage to Nova Scotia in ancient times. It is not possible to date stone carvings. I speculated many theories as to how they may have ended up being carved on that stone surface.

Some people have made suggestions based on personal conjectures that those hieroglyphs may have been carved in the early 1800's. For a time I had even entertained the date of 1881 because of an azimuth alignment with Oak Island and the "Cleopatra Needle" located in Central Park, New York, New York. There is a chart in this book showing more details as to that connection. That Cleopatra Needle Obelisk was erected on that location in Central Park in 1881. Very interesting! In my next book that I plan to publish in the near future that will be addressed in greater detail if all goes well. I am going to leave it like it is for now.

These 5 hieroglyphs are an unfinished work that represents the name of Queen "Cleopatra" of ancient Egypt. Here is the Terry J. Deveau report concerning the Egyptian Hieroglyphs as follows:

Terry mentions: "THE CLEOPATRA HIEROGLYPHIC." Check out this website: "Admiral Cove Park, Halifax County." Here you will see a very clear photo of the famous Bedford "Eagle Rock." Also, a map that shows the location of the "Cleopatra Hieroglyphics."

"G3 – I want to come back and discuss G3 because it is so different from all the others. It is the set of 5 hieroglyphic symbols labeled (1) on the web page referenced above. It is on a large flat, almost vertical rock face, at sea level, about chest high. The greywacke is quite hard at this location, but this rock face is also coated with a veneer of quartz, making it even harder. There once was a thin sheet/vein of quartz in the bedrock, a very large block broke off, leaving the quartz sheet exposed on the rock face. This carving is superb. The lines are crisp and clean, the curves are smooth and lovely. This is the work of a true professional. He chose a place where his work could be easily seen from the water, and would persist for a very long time. I don't know how one might date this inscription, but if someone told me that it was thousands of years old, I would have no problem believing it. It truly is remarkable, and unlike anything else I have seen in Nova Scotia.

"Except for one point of similarity with the Yarmouth Fletcher (Runic) stone: that stone also has its inscription carved onto a quartz veneer, over top of a Goldenville formation stone. It makes sense that an authentic inscription carver would want to carve his message on the very hardest stone he could find, so it would survive better, especially if it was at the edge of the ocean. I think this observation is significant, and bolsters the circumstantial evidence for the authenticity of both inscriptions. Pranksters, it would seem to me, would be happy to use less effort on softer stone. Indeed, the 5 hieroglyphics take up only a small area of the large vertical rock face, but despite all the other carvings on softer rock nearby, no one else took the effort required to carve on that quartz veneer. The hieroglyphics have that prime area all to themselves." (As posted on NEARA: New England Antiquities Research Association founded in 1964)

**Note:** I would like to make it perfectly clear that at no time did Terry J. Deveau of Halifax County Nova Scotia support or promote any of my own views of the Egyptians possibly landing on the shore of Nova Scotia in ancient times. - Jack Mac Nab

# Chapter 1

# Oak Island HO-Stone and the 90-Foot Inscribed Stone

The Oak Island HO-Stone was discovered in the early 1930's by Gilbert Hedden. Based on my own investigation, the characters inscribed on that stone are none other than Tifinagh, a script once used by the Berbers of North Africa. It is believed that these characters were carved into a much larger boulder which was once located somewhere along the shoreline of Joudrey's Cove on Oak Island. Someone got the idea that treasure might be hidden under that boulder, so they went ahead and dynamited it in hopes of finding priceless treasures. Disappointingly for those thoughtless treasure hunters, none was to be found. The HO-Stone is only a fragment of that much larger boulder that was destroyed.

There is a 1936 photo showing what that fragment of stone looked like, with those characters carved on its surface. I have attempted over the years to decipher that Berber inscription. My best decipherment has been accomplished by turning the characters shown in that photo upside-down.

To this very day, the question of whether or not there were more Berber characters carved on that much larger boulder remains unknown. Here are what the characters carved on the HO-Stone look like, when written in Neo-Tifinagh Script (Berber): ⊙⁚+⁚Ж. These characters, when I deciphered them, spell the word *"sutuf."* I was able to trace *"sutuf"* on Google Maps to a place-name in the

Western Sahara known as "Adrar Sutuf". (21°53'46.16"N 15°25'51.54"E)

## sutuf
## ⊙⁚+⁚Ⅱ

Remarkable! The inscription on Oak Island's HO-stone, written in a Berber script, designates a place in Africa's Western Sahara, the historic domain of the Berber people. Coincidence? I'm inclined to believe not.

The place-name Adrar Sutuf is a mountain range located in the Sahara Desert in Mauritania (Northwestern Africa). The Berbers (Amazigh) are indigenous to this area of North Africa, and their language is traditionally written with ancient Libyco-Berber Script, which now exist in the form of Tifinagh. (Modern term: Neo-Tifinagh)

It appears that we are looking at a transatlantic voyage from North Africa to Oak Island Nova Scotia possibly thousands of years ago. The Mahone Bay area, where Oak Island is situated, was in fact a *lagoon* 8,000 years ago. At one time, Oak Island was part of the mainland. With the continuous rising sea level due to the constant melting of the glaciers, it eventually transformed into an *island* during the passing of many hundreds of years.

Considering that the Mi'kmaq have lived on the soil of Nova Scotia for thousands of years, it seems likely to me that, if Berbers really travelled from North Africa to the shores of Nova Scotia in centuries past, the Mi'kmaq might have recorded these transatlantic voyages in their oral tradition. Perhaps the Mi'kmaq legend "Of Other Men who went to Glooscap for Gifts" is one such record. I am not claiming this to be a real *fact*; I am merely suggesting that this old Mi'kmaq tale *appears*, to me, to be a reference to one or more of these potential voyages. Who knows!

# The Berber Tifinagh Oak Island Script
(Jack Mac Nab 10/10/2020)

The Oak Island HO-Stone was discovered in the Jourdry's Cove area of Oak Island Nova Scotia in the early 1930's. There is a 1936 photo showing the inscription on this stone as being none other than Berber/Tifinagh Script. My decipherment is derived by means of turning that inscribed stone upside down and is deciphered in Neo-Tifinagh as "sutuf."

I was able to trace this name "sutuf" specifically to a location in the Western Sahara known as "Adrar Sutuf." It is a *fact* that the Berber/Amazigh language has been in use in the Western Sahara for many centuries.

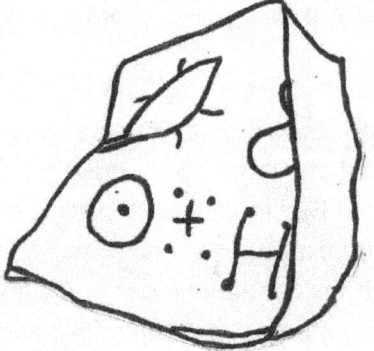

**Adrar Sutuf Western Sahara**
(21°53'46.16"N 15°25'51.54"W)

The Adrar Sotuf is a mountain range located in the Sahara Desert in northern Mauritania. The Berbers (Amazigh) are indigenous to North Africa and their language is traditionally written with ancient Libyco-Berber Script, which now exist in the form of Tifinagh. (A more modern term is known as Neo-Tifinagh)

| ⊙ - S | ⁝ - U | + - T | ⁝ - U | Ƕ - F |
|---|---|---|---|---|
| ⊙ | ⁝ | + | ⁝ | Ƕ |

**Oak Island HO-Stone**
(44°30'54.73"N 64°17'32.03")

## ⊙⁝+⁝Ƕ
## Sutuf

**Adrar Sutuf Western Sahara**
(21°53'46.16"N 15°25'51.54"W)

| Oklahoma Stone Carving Iberian Punic Script | HO-Stone Oak Island Nova Scotia | Indus Valley Script Harappen Civilisation |
|---|---|---|

13

# The Kempton Cipher

This chart is showing Kempton symbols that are believed to have been carved on the original inscribed Stone that was brought up from the 90-foot level in the famous Oak Money Pit in 1804. The Kempton Cipher was published in a book named "True Tales of Buried Treasure" by Edward Rowe Snow. (1949) It has been claimed that the decipherment of these symbols read as follows: "Forty Feet Below, Two Million Pounds are Buried." Prior to this decipherment most newspapers reported that it read "Ten Feet Below" and not "Forty Feet Below." As for me I do not buy into these claims.

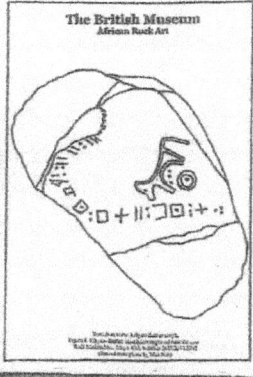

Berber/Neo/Tifinagh Script

··· O Θ + 8 Δ
q r s t u v

⊔ x ⌐⌐ ⌐
w x z y

Berber/Neo/Tifinagh Script

o Θ c Λ§ H X
a b c d e f g

⋮ Σ Ⅰ ⋮ Λ ⌐ Ⅰ o Ƨ
h i j k l m n o p

The British Museum
African Rock Art

(Jack Mac Nab 1/1/2017)

# Of Other Men who went to Glooscap for Gifts

(The Algonquin Legends of the New England States Index- Sacred Text;
Decipherment in brackets by author)

In old times (N'kah-ne-oo)
And it came to pass that a certain fool
Made a long journey (sea voyage)

To the Master (Somewhere in North America)
His trails were many (Via the Mediterranean Sea into the Atlantic)

He came to an exceedingly high mountain (Gibraltar)
Yet it was worse beyond (Atlantic Ocean/filled with sea-monsters)
For there the road lay between (Spain & Africa)
Two huge serpents (Two Pillars of Hercules)

Almost touching each other (Spain & Africa 8.8 mi./14.3 km.)
Who darted their terrible tongues (winds and currents of the Atlantic)
At those who went between (Pillars of Hercules)

And yet the path (Strait of Gibraltar)
Passed under the Wall of Death (Ships sailed through that strait)
Now this wall hung like an awful cloud (Darkness of Fog)

Over a plain (Flat surface of the Atlantic Ocean)
Rising and falling yet no man knew when (Rising and falling ocean tides)
That so as to crush (Ships being crushed by ocean waves)
All that went beneath. (Ships sailing through Strait of Gibraltar)

**Author:** It is not fully clear to me at this point in time who may have carved those characters on that HO-Stone in ancient times. Queen Scotia was my first option. My second option is a member of the Alexander Helios voyage. Time will tell.

All claims made in my book *Queen Scotia and the Egyptian Connection to Oak Island,* concerning the Queen Scotia's voyage from Egypt to Ireland and Scotland, are based on finding by Egyptologist Lorraine Evens in her book "Kingdom of the Ark." (2000)

All claims made in my book *Queen Scotia and the Egyptian Connection to Oak Island* concerning the Queen Scotia's voyage to Nova Scotia, have been inspired by the writings of John "Bear" MacNeil in his book *Basket Stories a Mi'kmaq Heritage Book.* (2014)

As for the Alexander Helios voyage to Nova Scotia, most of my claims are based on findings by Harry Hubbards and Paul Shaffranke, which were and still are posted on their Facebook Site: "The Illinois Caves." Most of these quotes in my book are from correspondence between myself and Harry and Paul from about 2010 to 2020.

## A: The Queen Scotia voyage to Nova Scotia, sometime after 1350 B.C.

To set the record straight in my book *Queen Scotia and the Egyptian Connection to Oak Island,* I had mentioned: "It is my belief that the Princess Scotia, who was none other than Princess Maritaten of the 18$^{th}$ Dynasty of Egypt, made a voyage to Scotland and Ireland in and about 1350 B.C. This mythological voyage is viewed by me and many others as being based on *fact*. My claim that Scotia made a transatlantic voyage to Nova Scotia in the latter part of the 14th Century B.C. should be viewed as a *mythological tale created by me*. Fact or fiction? Time will tell."

## B: The Alexander Helios voyage to Nova Scotia, sometime after 24 B.C.

At the time of writing the "Queen Scotia and the Egyptian Connection to Oak Island," I was fully aware of the claims made by Harry Hubbards and Paul Shaffranke that Alexander Helios and his younger brother, Ptolemy Philadelphus, made a voyage to Nova Scotia. They departed in a fleet of ships from the area of the Mississippi Delta, heading for Nova Scotia in the latter part of the 1st Century B.C.

## C:

It should also be mentioned that I never made any connections with Queen Scotia and the Mi'kmaq Hero Glooscap, who came to Nova Scotia from across the Atlantic Ocean. Others, but not me, have claimed that this Glooscap may have been the Norsemen, Prince Henry Sinclair, etc.

There was also a Glooscap that came up from the south via Maine to Nova Scotia. There was no connection with this Glooscap and Queen Scotia. Some people have suggested that this Glooscap might have some sort of connection with Quetzalcoatl, the legendary "Feathered Serpent" of Aztec mythology. I do not buy into that theory at all, and consider it one of the many tall-tales that continue to add to the Oak Island fake-folklore-news.

Final question: Could, the Hero Glooscap be none other than Alexander Helios? And could Glooscap's younger brother Malcom, be none other than Alexander Helios' younger brother, Ptolemy Philadelphus? This possibility will be investigated, but may never be proven as a real *fact* beyond a reasonable doubt.

## D:

It should be mentioned that Glooscap was the spiritual leader, chief and hero of the Mi'kmaq. The original Glooscap is said to have lived on Cape Breton Island, Nova Scotia, thousands of years ago. As mentioned earlier, I am inclined to believe there were other voyagers that came to Nova Scotia following that timeline. There appears to have been a corruption of many of the oral traditions of the Algonquin who lived in the Maritime Provinces of Canada and the New England States, etc. This corruption came about when the English and the French attempted to write these legends down on paper in the 1800's and earlier. What is real *fact* and *fiction* is for you, the reader, to decide. As for me, I find this kind of investigation to be highly interesting.

# Chapter 2

# The Queen Scotia Update

(She was not entombed at the bottom of the famous

Money Pit on Oak Island.)

This book that you are reading now should be viewed as an historical investigation on my part into who may have visited the shores of North America prior to 1492. Plato, in his writings *Timaeus* and *Critias* (4th Century B.C.), referred to a "Boundless Continent" that was on the opposite side of the Atlantic Ocean to the Straits of Gibraltar (North Africa). I believe this "Boundless Continent" to be none other than the Americas (North and South America). This book will be focused more specifically on North America.

In my most recently published book, *Queen Scotia and the Egyptian Connection to Oak Island* (2020), I had entertained the theory that Queen Scotia (Scota) made a voyage from Egypt to Ireland and Scotland in the 14th Century B.C.

At first, I viewed this voyage with a fair amount of skepticism until I read the book written by Egyptologist Lorraine Evens named *Kingdom of the Ark* (2000). According to Evens: "Princess Scota was none other than Princess Meritatan of the 18th Dynasty of Egypt, daughter of Pharaoh Akhenaten. It is claimed that Maritaten was expelled from her homeland in and about 1330-1300 B.C. After leaving Egypt, her people travelled to ancient Scythia, Spain, Britain, Ireland, and Scotland. It has been claimed that Ireland derived its name from the name 'Scota' after the Irish tribes colonized Scotland, and that country also bore her name."

**Author:** Scota is well known as Princes Scota and Queen Scota. Seeing where she is also known as "Scotia", I made the decision to refer to her in my book as *Queen Scotia*. It seemed to me that *Nova Scotia* may have originally got its name from *Queen Scotia*. Yet, that may not be a *fact* but only a coincidence.

It appeared to me that Queen Scotia may have spent a short period of time on the soil of Nova Scotia in the latter part of the 14$^{th}$ Century B.C., specifically Cape Breton Island. The first clue of Queen Scotia possibly being in Nova Scotia came from a book written by John "Bear" MacNeil, named *Basket Stories a Mi'kmaq Heritage Book* (2014).

According to MacNeil: "Queen Skatha, (Scotach, Sgota, Shatha) made a transatlantic voyage to the shores of Nova Scotia, and built a 'castle' in the Bras d'Or Lakes area of Cape Breton Island. At some point in time, a young man named Cuchulain (Koo-hoo-lin) entered into the service of 'Queen Skatha'…and Cuchulain crossed the Atlantic Ocean after a perilous sea voyage. Landed on the shores of Cape Breton Island and attended school for a year and a half in Queen Skatha's Castle…After Cuchulain finished his schooling in that castle on Cape Breton Island, he then returns to Ireland and marries Emer."

It is easy for me to see that Queen Skatha was none other than Queen Scotia. By means of changing a few letters, this connection becomes very obvious. The changing of letters is nothing new! As an example: The "C" in Canada changes to a "K" when being used in Europe. Hence: Kanada.

Scota can also be spelled as follows: "Scotia, Scot, Scoti, Scotii, Skota, Scuta."

Scota → Sgota → Scota → Scata-ch →

Scot-ia → Scat-ha → Skat-ha

I hazard to guess that Queen Scotia pulled away from the shores of Scotland in the latter part of the 14th Century B.C. She was headed for what is now known as North America. Her ships made their way past the Shetland Islands, Faroe Islands, Iceland, and Greenland, crossed over to Baffin Island or Labrador, and then made their way past Newfoundland until they spotted Nova Scotia, Canada.

I can only speculate that Queen Scotia made landfall in the Cape Breton area of Nova Scotia as claimed by John Paul MacNeil. It is very possible that she spent time on Scatarie Island, Cape Breton. It appears to me that the name "Scata" in the name of "Scata---rie" contains the name "Scota." For all we know maybe that island was named in her honour.

It should be mentioned that, according to Wikipedia: "Scott Cunningham speculates that the name Scatarie is thought to have originated with the Portuguese. It was possibly a whaling station...located on the eastern tip of Cape Breton Island, a large, irregular shaped island pointing its crooked finger across the ocean."

John Bear MacNeil believes that Cape Breton Island may have been named after Pharaoh Unas of ancient Egypt. Incredibly, there are two Mi'kmaq place-names for Cape Breton Island which resemble ancient Egyptian names. They are "Unama'kik" and "Onamag". Both mean "Land of Fog." The "Una" in Una---ma'kik and the "Ona" in Ona---mag appear to have a connection to the Egyptian name "Unas", as in Pharaoh. The Hellenized name for "Unas" is "Onas." The Hellenized name for the Mi'kmaq name Unama'kik is Onamag. (John Bear MacNeil *Basket Stories a Mi'kmaq Heritage Book*)

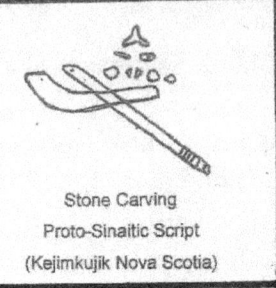

Stone Carving
Proto-Sinaitic Script
(Kejimkujik Nova Scotia)

No. 1: Characters from Keji stone carving tracing.

No. 2: Keji stone carving appear to represent these shapes.

No. 3: A variety of matching ancient characters.

## Chart 2

As early as 1881 George Creed of Nova Scotia discovered various stone carvings in the Kejimkujik area of Nova Scotia. Six years later in 1888 he and his wife with two nephews spent several weeks tracing these stone carvings. It is claimed that they discovered and traced several hundred petroglyphs. These tracing are now preserved in the Nova Scotia Museum in Halifax. The source of this tracing as shown on my chart is to be found in the book named: Rock Drawings of The Micmac Indians, by Marion Robertson in 1973. These tracings were reproduced by Lynda Peverill. (The Nova Scotia Museum)

(Jack Mac Nab 1/1/2017)

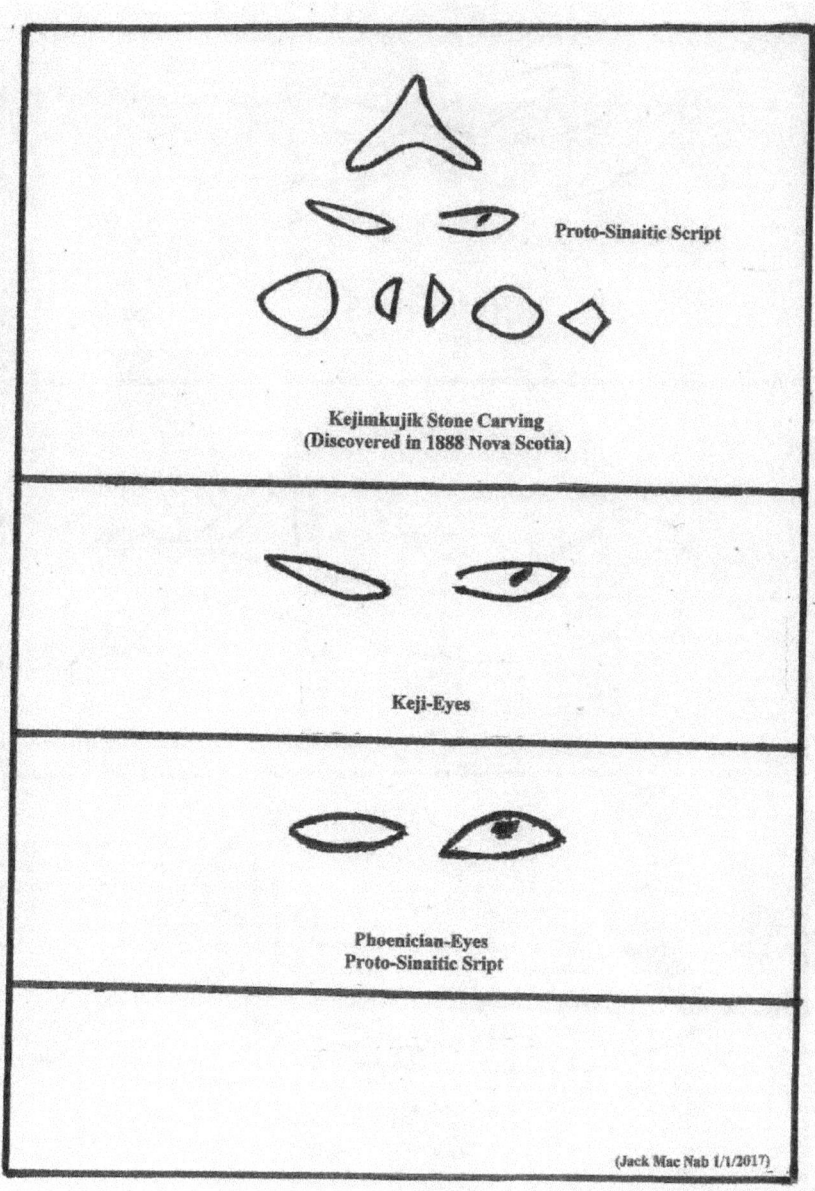

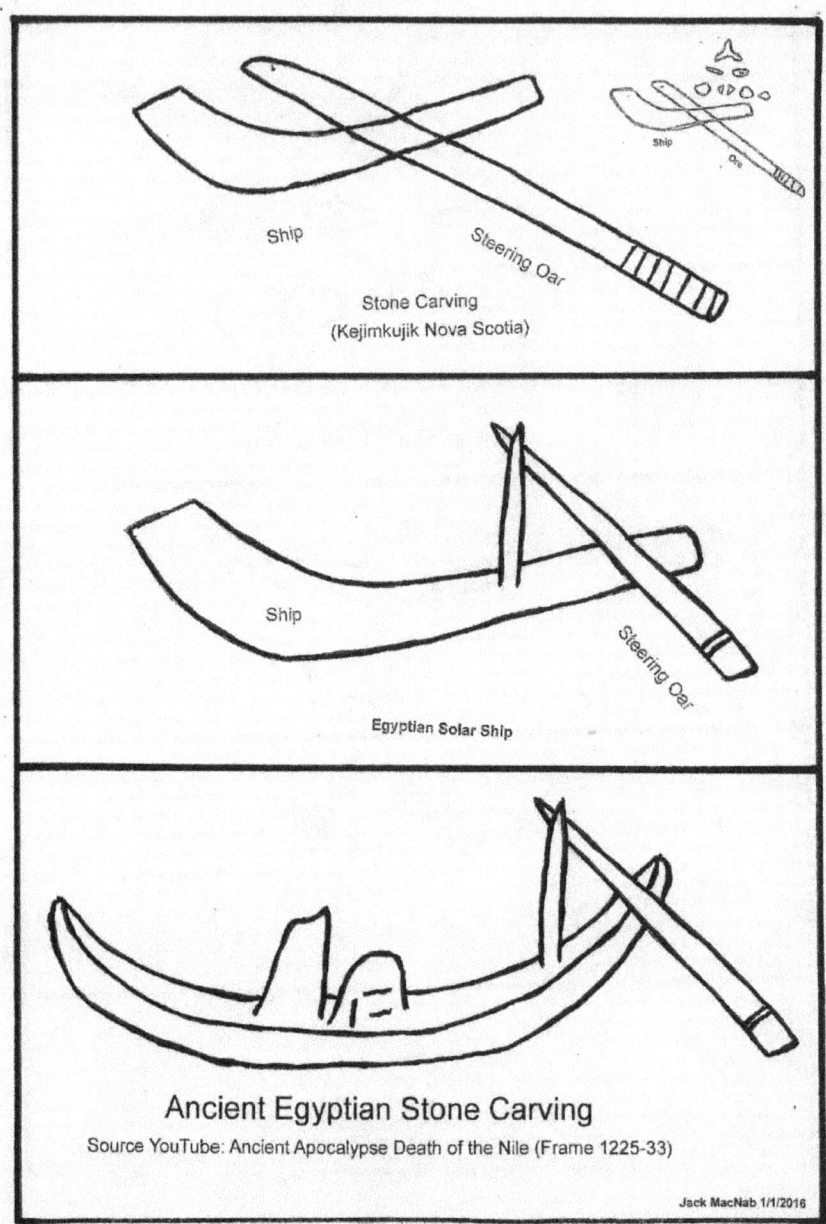

Stone Carving
(Kejimkujik Nova Scotia)

Egyptian Solar Ship

Ancient Egyptian Stone Carving
Source YouTube: Ancient Apocalypse Death of the Nile (Frame 1225-33)

Jack MacNab 1/1/2016

# Unama'kik or Onamag =
# Cape Breton Island (Land of Fog)

### Una in Unama'kik = Pharaoh Unas

Una---------ma'kik   (Mi'kmaq)  
Unas                (Pharaoh)

Una---------ma'gi   (Mi'kmaq)  
Unis                (Pharaoh)

### Hellenized name is Onas

Ona-------mag   (Mi'kmaq)  
Oenas            (Pharaoh)

Onama'gi      (Mi'kmaq)  
Onnos            (Pharaoh)

### Mi'kmaq        Egyptian Pharaoh

Cape Breton I. = Unas  
Unama'kik =    Unas  
Unama'gi  =    Unis

Hellenized name: Onas  
Onamag   =   Oenas  
Onama'gi  =   Onnos

     Also, in my book *Queen Scotia and the Egyptian Connection to Oak Island,* it is mentioned: "My findings about Princes Scota are based on Irish and Scottish mythology. As for my claim Queen Scotia (Scota) made a transatlantic voyage to Nova Scotia and Oak Island, this should *not* be viewed as a *fact* at this point in time. Maybe someday, more facts and artifacts will surface that will prove these claims to be so. For all we known it is *plausible* that Queen Scotia was entombed at the bottom of the famous Oak Island Money Pit. Who knows?" (Page 86)

To mention that it was *plausible* that Queen Scotia was entombed in that pit, is to be viewed only as being very suggestive. Yet, her claimed gravesite in located is Ireland. It is believed that Queen Scotia died in battle "while pregnant when she attempted to jump a bank on horseback." This battle is believed to have taken place in the Slieve Mish area sometime during the latter part of the 14th Century B.C. Her gravesite is very near to where she was killed in that battle. (Coordinates: 52°13'34.33"N 9°42'39.60"W)

According to Wikipedia: "The grave of Scotia (Scota) reputedly lies in a valley, south of Tralee town, in Co. Kerry, Ireland. The area is known as Glenn Scoithin 'Valley of the little flower', more normally known as Foley Glen. Indicated by a county council road signpost, a trail from the road leads along a stream to a clearing where a circle of large stones marks the grave site. Scotia's grave is reputed to be under a huge ancient stone inscribed with Egyptian hieroglyphs."

The Slieve Mish Mountains according to Wikipedia: "Overlooking Tralee Bay on the northern side and Dingle Bay on the south, they extend for approximately 19 km from east to west. They run from mainland just south of Tralee along the center of the neck of the Dingle Peninsula, before ending in a series of low foothills and deep river valleys which separate them from the Mountains of the central Dingle Peninsula further to the west. The mountain range is relatively narrow, extending only 7 km from north to south. The mountains from a high ridge of sandstone which was deeply incised by glaciers in the last ice age leaving behind U-shaped valleys and Corrie Lakes." (Locks) (Page 107)

**Author:** My main point! Queen Scotia was not buried or entombed at the bottom of the famous Money Pit located on Oak

Island, Nova Scotia. She was buried or entombed at in that claimed location known as "Foley Glen" in Ireland.

# Chapter 3

## The Marion County Illinois Caves Discovery

The following information about the Marion County Illinois Cave discovery is mostly derived from various discussion that took place between Harry Hubbart, Paul Shaffranke and myself on the Facebook site *"The Illinois Caves."* This sharing of information all began shortly after I moved from Nova Scotia, Canada, to Austria in 2010. The following illustrates the timeline of the events that unfolded after the discovery of that cave located in Marion County Illinois.

## **1925**

**Harry Hubbards:** "In spring of 1925, a local resident, Orville Lowery, of Hickory Hill, in the southeast corner of Marion County, Illinois, was busy with his two daughters removing rocks and debris from an area designated to be the family garden. His eldest daughter, Fern, who was six years old, began to explore along the ledge of the ravine next to the garden spot. Several feet away from the bluff, Fern discovered a hole, cut through the sandstone by human hands. She called her father over to investigate the hole which he determined was of ancient origin.

"Orville worked diligently for years attempting to get professional investigators from the state of Illinois out to the site to examine this entrance into the subterranean cavity. Orville was met with futility as the Illinois experts sloughed off the idea that anything of ancient significance could possibly exist in the most remote regions of Marion County. However, Orville was able to get Fern's discovery recorded in the WPA journals in Salem, the county seat. Frustrated for lack of interest, Orville later sold his property and moved to Mt. Vernon about 20 miles away in the early 1930's, taking with him his two charming girls. Fern and her sister grew up in Mt. Vernon, got married and moved to different states forsaking all prior knowledge of their family discovery. Orville likewise ceased to pursue attempting to arouse the bitter scholars who had neglected him so many times."

## **1961**

**Harry (cont.):** "All was quiet for decades, until one balmy day in early summer of 1961 when Michael Paul Henson, the most famous treasure guide writer in the country, approached Orville after reading about the discovery in the Salem courthouse. Excited at the renewed interest, Orville met with Henson and escorted him to the site of the ancient portal.

"Henson, the respected writer of lost treasure books, published the information he had obtained in subsequent releases. Others who often copied Henson's work also duplicated this twisted tale of discovery long after the death of Orville in 1974."

## **1982**

**Harry (cont.):** "In April of 1982, a Redneck from Olney, Illinois crisscrossed the coordinates of different treasure guides published years before in order to relocate the ancient portal."

# 1994

**Harry (cont.):** "It is here that our story begins! We became involved with the Lowery Cave Project in summer of 1994. Since that time, dozens of people have been searching for the entrance that the former Olney resident covered up...etc."

# 2010

**Author:** In about 2010, I took and interest the Illinois Cave discovery. That was the year that I moved from Bedford, Nova Scotia, to Klagenfurt, Austria. I had been surfing the Internet in search of any discoveries that might have a possible connection to my various stone carving discoveries that I made in Bedford Basin area of Nova Scotia between the years of 1985 to 1992.

It was in about 2010 that I came across "The Illinois Caves" Facebook site that was set up by Harry Hubbards and Paul Schaffranke. Within a short period of time, we began exchanging information, photos, theories, claims, etc.

During the past couple of years our interaction had tapered off a bit for no real outstanding reason. It was not until I had published my book named "Queen Scotia and the Egyptian Connection to Oak Island" that we reconnected. (Published on Amazon Books by Hammerson Peters 2020)

# 1994 - 2020

**Harry Hubbards and Paul Schaffranke:** "Since about 1994, they had obtained 100's of stone carvings that are claimed to have come out of that Marion County Cave, plus, view 100's owned by other people. They have reached the conclusion by deciphering many of these writings that this Marion County Cave contained the Sema of the Ptolemaic Dynasty."

# Chapter 4

# The Marion County Illinois Caves Discovery Explained

What you will read in this following information is what is posted on "The Illinois Caves" Facebook site for all to read.

**Harry Hubbards:** "During the Hellenistic Age, a great dynasty rose up to rule over the land of Egypt. King Alexander the Great of Pella, who had conquered all the wealth of the known world, established the city of Alexandria, and died in Babylon. On the return trip to Macedonia, his body was commandeered by his first General and half-brother, Ptolemy. Ptolemy showed off the elaborate coffin first in Memphis and then moved the cadaver to Alexandria where he would enshrine it after the new mausoleum was completed. At Alexandria, Ptolemy established the Dynasty Sema adjacent to the new museum. A library was also being built in the new complex. These and other facts are recorded textbook history.

"As a result, the Ptolemaic Dynasty was created. This Dynasty became the curators of all the knowledge of the world, the largest collection of ancient artifacts and the largest library in history. They also possessed a horde of gold so immense; it would have required a caravan of wagons one mile in length to transport it from one place to another. Ptolemy (Soter I) dedicated a proportioned parcel of land in the heart of the city especially, to accommodate all this vast wealth and knowledge.

"After over 250 years, the Dynasty finally yielded to the

Roman Empire, but not before the Ptolemies had acquired the many tons of gold and silver, the finest jewels, the most prized maps and books with the most magnificent museum on Earth. All of it now belonged to Emperor Octavian and the Roman Empire. Octavian made a leisure trip one day to view his newfound wealth after Alexandria fell into his hands. He truly enjoyed seeing the museum with its artifacts and books, but most particular, his visit to the Ptolemaic Tomb on the west side of the lot. The Tomb was soon to be host of three new bodies, two of which were already designated. Just days after his arrival, Queen Cleopatra VII and her youngest brother, Ptolemy XIII were added to the eternal members of this marbled mausoleum for the Royal Dead. Octavian swiftly passed by this crypt as well as all the other crypts containing the Kings of this Dynasty. Octavian went directly to the Main Crypt where King Alexander the Great lay enshrined forever. Octavian silently stood gazing and glassy-eyed: King Alexander the Great, in his solid alabaster sarcophagus with a glass cover – Alexander, with his Famous Trojan Shield and gold Death Mask. Octavian became fixated and remained there for many hours in awe. His general nudged him to break the spell and said, 'Ptolemy I, is entombed just over there. Would you care to view it?'

"Octavian looked up at him and said, 'I came to see a King, not a corpse.' History also records that for some strange reason Octavian touched or struck the nose of Alexander and damaged it. What made him do this? Was the Death Mask on Alexander? Where was the gold sarcophagus, he had heard so much about? Could it be he noticed after studying the body long enough, he was staring at a cenotaph? After a few moments, Octavian turned, left the tomb and shortly thereafter, he left Egypt and returned to Rome. Little did he realize he would be the last person recorded in history as having actually been in the presence of this Tomb. This Royal Tomb, with all its splendor and gold, vanished along with a great portion of the contents in the museum and hundreds of volumes from the library.

"From the evidence gathered by deciphering the tablets of script found in the Lost Tomb of Alexander the Great, it is now possible to present for the first time a portion of forgotten history beginning as follows:

"There was a captured Carthaginian prince living under the stewardship of Octavian, who also served in Octavian's army, Juba, son of King Juba I (pronounced as 'you – bah'). King Juba I of Mauretania had been defeated at Thalpsus by Julius Caesar and butchered because of his alliance with Pompey during the Civil Wars. The dead king's son was taken hostage and in later years distinguished himself greatly. Juba was deeply admired by the emperor Octavian. There was a great dilemma for Octavian with regard to the treatment of Marc Antony's remaining legions who had surrendered to him following the battle of Actium. There was no more land available in Italy or on the frontier available for the Antonian veterans, who were the highly skilled elite warriors of the Roman army. This included Julius Caesar's famous and powerful Tenth Legion. Antony's army hated Octavian and had no desire to fight in his army. Octavian's highest priority was to provide for his own soldiers first. He had even less desire for large numbers of former hostile forces to remain in his empire. We know from history Octavian demobilized his army of 60 legions down to 24.

"The young captive Juba must have eventually come up with an answer to this great problem for Octavian. The Mauretanians had knowledge of a centuries old Phoenician / Carthaginian colony a great distance to the west of the 'Pillars of Hercules'. This land had been recorded by ancient authors as being rich with rivers, gold, copper, and was also the source of the famous Purpur used to make dye. Diodorus Sicullus, Pliny and others, give reference to this land beyond the ocean. Juba was a brilliant man and aware of what was known through legend as 'Happyland' or the *Land of Many Smiles*. Juba suggested to the emperor that he should build Mauretanian ports along the Atlantic coast and fortify the Port of Gades in Spain. Juba explained how the mighty Emperor could extend his trade into the heartland of Spain traveling up the Baetis River and digging a canal through the vast marshland along its northern bank. He also suggested the Antony's legions with their great fleet be sent to this colony in order to conquer, settle, and start anew the flow of goods from there back to the Roman Empire.

"Juba's idea was a great solution, for not only could Octavian get rid of Antony's army, but he could also employ them to send him large quantities of copper which could be mixed with his tin from Britain. Juba's plan received Octavian's approval and Juba was made monarch of both Numidia and Mauretania as a reward. The now King Juba II was placed in charge of supervising the operation.

"In 28 BC, a large fleet which included many remnants of the Actium fleet, comprised of at least two legions, warships of the trireme and quinquereme type with many transports for supplies and small riverboats, set sail from the Port of Tingis (Tingi). They were commanded by Admiral Sosius who had served under the leadership of Antony. The first fleet consisted of 67 ships and only one was lost at sea.

"The armada arrived in the land to the west directly translated as The Land of Many Smiles or called by slang, Happyland, about a month after its departure. They colonized settlements in the vicinity of the Florida panhandle, Cuba, the Bahama Islands and penetrated up the Alabama River (which is referred to as the 'White River') and farther on to the regions northward. In about 26 BC, these settlers began migrating up the Mississippi River, they called the 'Great and Mighty Water-Flow' where they allied with the former inhabitants of the Carthaginian Empire. They established a major city and port near present day St. Louis and called it 'Caesarea, the City of the Sun.' This site can still be viewed today known as the Cahokia Mounds. These North African descendants controlled most of the settlements along the Mississippi, Tennessee, and Ohio River basins.

"They attempted to reach the Michigan copper country overland in order to reestablish the copper trade, when they met disaster at the hands of the Natives consisting of large numbers of the "Horned Helmets" and "Stinkards" (or 'bad-smelling people').

"Back in time to the Mediterranean Sea, following the defeat and alleged suicides of Mark Antony and the mother of his three surviving children, Queen Kleopatra VII, the three royal siblings: Alexander Helios, Cleopatra Selene (who were twins) and Ptolemy Philadelphus were chained and returned to Rome. Octavian paraded them in gold cages at his triumph celebration, and their mother was represented by a life-sized golden image of herself lying on a couch.

"The children were raised in the palace by the emperor's sister, Octavia, who was Mark Antony's legal wife under Roman Law. Octavia regarded herself as the true mother of Antony's children and cared for them in the manner their custom would provide, while her brother, Octavian, (later called Augustus Caesar) was childless and regarded himself as the children's true uncle. Octavian was deeply concerned their future would be provided for in a noble fashion.

"The captive prince Juba and the much younger Selene fell in love after only a few years. Thus, began one of the most bizarre, romantic and forgotten love stories of all time. The Emperor admired the noble and loyal Juba, granting him back his homeland, changing his name to King Juba II and giving him the hand of Selene, his adopted niece.

"About 24 BC, the Mauritanian King Juba II married Cleopatra Selene, the daughter of Mark Antony and

Cleopatra. She then became known as Queen Cleopatra Selene of Mauretania. Both of her brothers, Alexander Helios and Ptolemy Philadelphus ended up in Mauretania also. With the new discoveries from the Lost Tomb of Alexander the Great, we can begin to piece together a portion of history which has been lost.

"From the famous ancient port at Gades off the southern coast of Spain, as well as ports along the Mauritanian coast, King Juba II expanded trade from North Africa to the British Isles and down the west coast of Africa. Since Juba was of royal blood, he had no problem becoming the administrator of what was left of the Carthaginian/Phoenician merchant fleet. We have determined Juba II, with the help of his wife Selene and brother-in-law Alexander Helios, was able to control and maintain the black-market goods being shipped from the east and transported down the Nile. This marketing network had been established several centuries before and with the sudden death of Cleopatra VII, there was no one supervising this "silk road" for a few years. It appears Juba II, having traveled the Nile as well as several countries beyond Arabia, was first in line for the overlord position.

"Commodities were in short supply but the demand for goods was constantly increasing. Juba II used his main port "Ioh Hyssar" at Caesarea, for his primary network hub. His ships sailed all over the Atlantic from this port. The insignia or trademark from this port has been found throughout the North American Continent. The famous port city of Ioh Hyssar was commuted from and to other ports such as Gades, Naples and the British Isles.

"Sometime during his early manhood, Alexander Helios voyaged to "Happyland" across the sea bringing with him the Sema of his ancestors. His ship traversed the river we know today as the Mississippi from the Gulf of Mexico. At the mouth of the present-day Ohio River, they took the eastern river route because it was twice as wide as the river flowing from the north. They continued their journey along the course of the main river, passing large tributaries, including the Tennessee and Cumberland Rivers. When they reached a large river flowing from the north, they left the main river and turned against the flow up the Wabash River. After traveling about 15 miles, they navigated westward up the Little Wabash River into an unknown territory. Traveling about 32 more miles, they somehow decided to traverse up a river known today as the Skillet Fork; most likely during the spring floods.

"We know Helios became a powerful king here in Happyland. The recorded evidence will show how the armies of Helios engaged a host of enemies from Illinois to Michigan, up into Lower Canada and eastward all the way back to the coastal islands near Maine and eastern Canada. We now have records written in stone which give details of battles fought in North America over 2000 years ago, complete with accurate maps and engaged infantry numbers.

"Alexander Helios was the first Sun King of Happyland and was adored by his people. He became a High Priest and was later deified as a god. Helios was a great warrior and general. He was killed later in life by wounds sustained during a battle and entombed near the location of his last victory. Helios, Juba II, Selene, Octavia and Queen Cleopatra VII along with their achievements, are forgotten no longer. The accomplishments of these five personages will live on in memory forever."

**Author:** Now that material explains in great detail what the Marion County Cave is all about, here are a few more points that I would like to draw your attention to.

There is a photo of an inscribed stone that came out of that Marion County cave that I believe is named "The Helios Death Tablet." The caption below Stone Tablet reads as follows:

"This is an excellent practice tablet for anyone familiar with the Schaff Alphabet. Paul Schaffranke deciphered this tablet in late fall of 1994.

"You will notice a picture-type, blemish of an image carved towards the center of the second section of text, which happens to be correctly oriented per the image above. There are dozens of tablets that contain fossils embedded within the stone medium. As was discovered, a fossil was often times used as a representation in the text.

"A typical account of such would be the often-used fossil Icons as representing mountains, volcanoes and natural landmarks. Upon many occasions, the fossil itself would be tampered with and disfigured (slightly or severely) to portray an image in relief, and exquisitely executed; as is the tablet here. The above tablet has had the embedded fossil slightly modified into an image of the "Island" the script relates to.

"The Island indicated on this tablet has an outline of the location where King Alexander Helios is entombed. There are a series of 3 tablets that describe the details of the final battle in which Helios-Rex ("King" in Latin) was severely wounded and died several days after his victory.

"In several years, possibly 4 to 10, we will speak about this stone like an old friend. We have no idea of the size of this tablet. It appears to be Lavangnia imported from Italy; 2000 years ago."

Harry and Paul believe that this "final battle" took place somewhere on the east coast of Canada in the general area of the Maritime Provinces. They felt at that time this elephant-shaped "Island" may have been the Island of Newfoundland. But they were not firm on reaching that conclusion. It was my suggestion that this "island" may possibly have been none other than Oak Island, Nova Scotia.

From what I understand, a fleet of ships pulled away from the Mississippi Delta area and prepared to do "battle" with the "Celts of Canada." Point of interest! The Mississippi Delta is on the same identical latitude line as the Great Pyramid of Giza.

**Paul Schaffanke:** "Helios invasion force had at most 2000 men and less than 50 trireme type ships at the time of the battle for Nova Scotia. The ships were also rebuilt locally. This expedition must have taken a couple of years. Start from Mobile Bay, round Florida and then make winter camp around Charleston S.C. Next spring rebuild ships and make it around Boston or Portsmouth N.H.

"Repeat this again the following year and the expedition arrives around Halifax, to capture the critical port where the river going and coast hugging type of ships would have to meet the deep-water ocean crossing vessels to transfer the copper and other goods for shipment to Europe.

"That accomplished, alliances were forged with local natives, to eventually muster some type of counter attack, but were ambushed in that battle mentioned previously. Oak Island Money Pit probably has all the answers!"

# Chapter 5

# Of Glooscap and his Younger Brother, Maslum

(The Algonquin Legends of the New England States – Index)

What you are about to read in this chapter should *not* be viewed as an absolute *fact*, but rather suggestion. My story is based on circumstantial evidence and bit of cherry picking. For many years, people have attempted to decipher the true nature and origin of Glooscap. I have no problem believing that there was an original Glooscap, who was the hero spiritual leader of the Mi'kmaq of Nova Scotia, Canada. It appears to me that things became corrupted over the centuries when explorers would land on the shores of Nova Scotia and were viewed by the Mi'kmaq as being a Glooscap who returned to his people from across the Atlantic Ocean.

## Glooscap and his Stone Canoe

The great lord
And creator was Glooscap
Where he was himself born
And when no man knows

From the place of his birth
He sailed across the sea
In a great stone canoe

To the part of America nearest the sun
He landed on the eastern shores of Canada
Far out he anchored his canoe
And it was so large that it became an island
And great trees grew on it

Far across the great sea
That he was the divine being
Though in the form of a man
He was not far from any of the Indians.
Glooscap was a friend and teacher of the Indians.

    According to the oral tradition of the Algonquin, Glooscap had a "younger brother named Malsum" (Malsumsis). This legend was recorded by Silas T. Rand and then Charles Leland in the 1800's.

    Could it be possible that the Glooscap described in this legend was none other than Alexander Helios? Could it also be possible that Glooscap's younger brother, Malsum, was none other than Helios' younger brother, Ptolemy Philadephus? I personally do not have a solid answer for those two questions. What I am saying is that it is very *plausible,* and I believe it is well worth researching.

    It is clearly understood that "Malsum" is definitely not a Mi'kmaq name. It a foreign name that originated somewhere else in North America. Malsum was viewed in these legends as being Gloocap's "twin" brother. It is very possible that the Native people heard that Alexander Helios had a "twin". This was not Ptolemy Philadephus, but rather his fraternal twin, Clepatra Selene (II). Maybe the truth will never really be known. Whatever the case, it sure is an interesting coincidence.

# How Glooscap made/Elves/Fairies/Man of Ash Tree/Coming at the Last Day

(The Algonquin Legends of the New England States – Index)

The reason why some of the ancient legends by the Algonquin appear to not make sense is because they were corrupted by the French and English during the translation process. Words placed in brackets are my decipherments.

Glooscap came first of all into this country
Into Nova Scotia
Maine
Into the land of the Wabanaki

Now the great lord Glooscap (Alexander Helios)
Who was worshiped,
In all the after-days
By all the Wabanaki
Or children of light

Was a twin (Alexander Helios' paternal twin was Selene)
With a brother (Ptolemy Philadephus)
(It appears that there was a mix-up and Ptolemy was viewed as the twin)

As he was good (Alexander Helios)
This brother name was Malsumsis (Ptolemy Philadephus)
Or Wolf the Younger. (Helios younger brother)
Was bad.

**Note:** There are a few things in these legends that would not have anything to do with Alexander Helios and Ptolemy Philadephus. For example, Malsum killed his mother and wanted to kill Glooscap. The real Ptolemy Philadephus never killed his mother Cleopatra VII, nor did he ever wish to kill his older brother Alexander Helios (Glooscap).

# The following is a footnote by Charles Leland.

(Words placed in brackets are my own decipherments)

He (Glooscap)
Will arise in the last day
When Glooscap (Alexander Helios)
Is to do battle
With the giants
And evil beast of olden time
And he will be the great destroyer
Glooscap is killed (Helios is killed in a battle with the Celts of Canada)

**Footnote:** Beneath this original legend by Charles Lelan, a footnote reads: "Malsum typifies destruction and sin in several of these tales. He will arise at the last day, when Glooscap is to do *battle* with all the *giants* and evil beasts of olden time, and will be the great destroyer."

According to Charles Leland, based on the oral tradition of the Algonquin, it is believed that the *"Stone Giants"* came to Canada as an army from the United States via the Niagara Falls area (Great Lakes). It is not clear to me where they were headed for when in Canada, nor do I know the motive for their migration. Maybe they were defending the cooper mining operations that are claimed to have taken place in the Great Lakes area in ancient times. Maybe someday we will know the whole story.

According to Harry and Paul, Alexander Helios, along with his younger brother, left in ships from the Mississippi Delta to Nova Scotia to do battle with the Celts of Canada in the general area of Nova Scotia. Could it be that the *"Giants"* mentioned in this legend were possibly the Celts of Canada? Is it even *plausible* that these "Stone Giants" were none other than the "Horned

Helmets" and "Stinkards" mentioned on those tablets that were retrieved from that Marion County Cave? Time will tell.

**Facebook site "The Illinois Cave" mentions:** "These North African descendants controlled most of the settlements along the Mississippi, Tennessee and Ohio River basins. They attempted to reach the Michigan copper country overland in order to reestablish the copper trade, when they met disaster at the hands of the Natives consisting of large numbers of the "Horned Helmets" and "Stinkards" (or 'bad-smelling people').

# Chapter 6

# Oak Island and the Temple of Umglebemu

(My claims concerning Umglebemu should be viewed as an investigation and not a proven fact. Maybe someday more facts and artifacts will surface to prove this story to be a fact beyond a reasonable doubt.)

While sharing information with Harry and Paul, I had suggested: "A couple of other likely places that these ships could possibly let down anchors based on my own finding is the general area of Penobscot, Maine." I had reached this conclusion based on the oral tradition of the Penobscot. (The Algonquin Legends of New England)

Chapter 7 in my book *Queen Scotia and the Egyptian Connection to Oak Island* explains why it appears to me that the Egypto-Romans may have constructed a "Temple" in the Penobscot area of Maine. According to oral tradition, someone had constructed a "Temple" that was named "Umglebemu" in the general area of the Sandy Point Game Management Area.

This Temple appears to have been constructed prior to the battle between the forces of Alexander Helios and the Celts of Canada in the Nova Scotia area. I am inclined to believe Helios was well aware of this "Temple." When he arrived in the Peneobscot River area, he discovered that the Temple of Umglebemu had been destroyed by an earthquake. It was then that Helios "king" (Rex) constructed the lost City of Norumbega. This city was constructed to stand for all time as a reminder of the destroyed Temple of Umglebemu. It may also have been constructed to be used, as Paul suggested, for the fleet of "ships [that] were also rebuilt locally" in preparation for the "Battle with the Celts of Canada."

It has been claimed that the Norse settlement in Newfoundland at L'Anse aux Meadows was used as a "winter boat repair station." It was named "Hop" and it is now believed by certain archaeologists that there was more than just one "Hop" located in the Maritime Provinces of Canada- possibly several "winter boat repair stations."

Oak Island    44°30'54.70" N 64°17'32.05"W

Odom Ledge 44°30'54.70" N    68°48'3.74"W

In ancient times, the "Temple of Umglebemu" is believed to have been located in Penobscot area of Maine. I have wondered about the meaning of the name "Umglebemu" for a very long time. It appears to me that the name "Umglebemu" may have been transmitted to Penobscot via Romans who possibly lived in that area of Maine in ancient times. I cannot prove this possibility beyond a reasonable doubt. At this point in time, I will present this information as being *fictional-thinking* on my part, until additional information comes forward that proves this hypothesis to be *fact*.

One thing we do know is that Umglebemu is referred to as a "Temple" (Templum). The Algonquin Legends of New England reveals that this "Temple of Umglebemu" was destroyed by a "massive earthquake." This "Temple" is claimed to have been replaced by a "castle" that was built by a "king." And that replacement "castle" was named "Norumbega." One might conclude that the name Norumbega is the decipherment of the name Umglebemu. I believe that is a real good possibility.

The "bega" in Norumbega may have been spelled "biga" meaning "Biga" as in the Biga Peninsula where Troy was located in ancient Greece. That peninsula was also known as Troas.

Knowing as I did that Norumbega appears to be a Roman place-name, it occurred to me "Umglebemu" would also be a Roman place-name! The letters "um" or "mu" at the beginning and at the end of "Um-glebe-mu" might very well be the clue to unlock this secret! It just so happened that when I was visiting Croatia (June 2015), I had stopped into a town named "Umag." The "Um" in "Um-ag" appeared to have the same meaning or sound as the "Um" in Um-glebe-mu! After doing a search of the name Umag, I did find out that it was part of the Old Roman Empire. After making that connection, I felt that I was headed in the right direction. I also came to realize that the two letters "um" were to be found in many ancient Roman place-names.

Next, I had decided to separate the letters as follows: "Um-----glebe-----mu." What caught my eye were the letters "g-l-e-b-e." Then it occurred to me that I once lived in a suburb in Ottawa, Canada, known as the Glebe. "The Glebe" is a subdivision located near Carleton University in Ottawa. At this point, it occurred to me that the letters "glebe" in Umglebemu had a true reliable name-place meaning as follow:

The Law Dictionary defines the meaning of "glebe" as follows:

1. In Roman Law: "glebe" means: a clod; turf; soil. Hence: the soil of an inheritance an agrarian estate.

2. In ecclesiastical law: "glebe" means: The land possessed as part of the endowment or revenue of a church.

I find it reasonable to conclude that this "Temple" was built on a special lot of land. That piece of "land" would serve as a sanctuary of some sort for the Roman Templum. (Glebe-Land) The "um" in Um-glebe-mu appears to have a connection with the Roman place-name "Camulodunum" (Ca--mu--lodun--um).

Wikipedia mentioned: Camulodunum is the Roman place-name for Colchester in Essex, England. (Latin: CAMVLODVNUM)

"The Ancient Roman name for what is now Colchester in Essex was an important town in Roman Britain, and served as the first capital of the province. It is claimed to be the oldest town in Britain... The Roman town began life as a Roman legionary base constructed in the AD 40's on the site of the Celtic fortress following its conquest by the Emperor Claudius... The town was home to a large classical temple, two theatres (including Britain's largest), several Romano-British temples...etc." (Wikipedia)

Wikipedia draws our attention to this interesting description: "The Temple of Claudius (TEMPLVM CLAVDII) or Temple of the Deified Claudius (TEMPLVM DIVI CLAVDII) was a large octastyle temple built in Camulodunum, the modern Colchester in Essex. The main building was constructed between 49 CE and 60 CE, although additions were built throughout the Roman era. Today, it forms the base of the Norman Colchester Castle. It is one of at least eight Roman era pagan temples in Colchester, and was the largest Temple of its kind in Roman Britain; its current remains potentially represent the earliest existing Roman stonework in the country.

"Construction of the temple began during Claudius' reign, and was dedicated to him after his death in 54 CE, with the official name of the town becoming "Colonia Claudia Victricensis" (The City of Claudius' Victory) and the temple becoming the "Templum Divi Claudii" (The Temple of the Deified Claudius). It was the centre for the Imperial Cult in the province...etc." (Wikipedia)

Wikipedia mentions that "after the earthquake, the old temple was claimed by the Penobscot, being previously on the Passamaquoddy side of the river. The "king" of the Penobscot turned it into a royal castle. Formerly called the Temple of Umglebemu, it was renamed Norumbega by the Penobscots...etc."

The Roman (Latin) word for Temple is "Templum." Hence, Umglebemu may have been known in ancient times as the Templum-on-the-Glebe-mu. It appears to me that Odum Island (also known as 'Glebe Island') would fit the description of the "Glebe"- as mentioned, a patch of "clod, turf, or soil" designated an "agrarian estate"- on which the Romans built a Templum to serve as a representation of their Empire in ancient America.

-----------um----------------glebe---mu
Templ---um----------------glebe---mu
Templ---um---(on the)---glebe---mu

Did the Temple of Umglebemu have a connection with the Temple of Claudius built in Camulodunum, in modern Colchester in Essex, England? At this point in time, I cannot confirm that it was or was not. Yet, I have reason to believe that both temples were in operation in and about that same time period in history.

**Author:** When I was attempting to decipher the names Umglebemu and the replacement castle "Norumbega", I had not made a connection with Norumbega and Alexander Helios the "King" (Rex) and his men. Yet my decipherment of the name Norumbega does seem give a few small hints that there is a connection. It is possible that the "bega" in Norum-bega may have been spelled "biga", a reference to the Biga Peninsula where Troy was located in ancient Greece. That peninsula was also known as Troas.

Alexander the Great was born in Pella, Greece, in 356 B.C., an ancient city located in Central Macedonia, which served as the capital of the Kingdom of Macedon at that time. Pelly was promoted to a Roman Colony sometime between 45 and 30 B.C. Hence: Noricum-biga. (The plausibility of this connection does not make it a *fact*. Just something to think about.)

# Chapter 7

# History of Oak Island, Nova Scotia, Since 1795

The following information concerning the history of Oak Island is based on a lot of folklore passed down from approximately 265 years to the present day. There are two large and two small drumlins located on Oak Island. Drumlins are elongated, oval shaped hills made up of various layers of bedrock, usually composed of what is known as Ordovician Halifax slate formations. It is claimed that about 8-10,000 years ago, Oak Island was part of a large lagoon that encompassed most of the Mahone Bay area. At that time, Oak Island was *not an island,* but was instead connected to the mainland. There is no doubt in my mind that the Old Gold River made its way through this lagoon near the location of present-day Oak Island. The old river bed is clearly visible on the bottom of that bay by means of side-scan-sonar equipment. (Oak Island: 44°30'54.70"N 64°17'32.05"W)

The name "Oak Island" has been revered by treasure hunters the world over. The ongoing treasure-hunt with which it is associated has lasted more than 200 years. During those years, six lives have been lost, and yet the elusive treasure has never been found. Various famous people have been involved in this relentless pursuit, such as Franklin D. Roosevelt, Errol Flynn, and John Wayne.

Oak Island had borne many names throughout its long and colourful history. It was originally named Gloucester Isle on a 1776 survey map of the Mahone Bay area (Royal Sound), drawn by J.F.W. Des Barres. The island was, for many years, known to mainlanders as Smith's Island.

What makes the Oak Island mystery so hard to solve is the fact that many of the artifacts that had been discovered on that island have disappeared over the years. It is very possible that many hidden secrets of Oak Island may never be known.

This quest for treasure all started back in 1795, when Daniel McGinnis from the Mahone Bay area discovered a bowl-shaped depression in the ground at the south-eastern end of the island. This circular depression was about 13-feet in diameter. Before long, Daniel and his two friends. John Smith and Anthony Vaughan, started excavating this strange depression in the ground. They were not boys at that time but instead three young men.

They dug down about 2-feet and uncovered a layer of carefully laid flagstones. This was of a type of stone not found on the island, and must have been transported from Gold River, about 2 miles north of the island on the mainland. Flagstone is a generic flat stone, and is usually a form of sandstone. In many cases flagstone was used for walkways, floors, roofs, etc.

It is now believed that the location of this "depression in the ground" was known for at least 40 years prior to this 1795 discovery by these three young men, pushing back the timeline to about 1755.

At a depth of 10-feet, McGinnis, Smith, and Vaughan struck a platform of oak logs that extended across the pit, with the ends securely embedded in the mud walls. These logs were 6 to 8 inches in diameter, strong enough to support 10-feet of soil. The young men continued digging past this location until they came to another oak platform on the 20-foot level. They continued to dig down, until they discovered another oak floor on the 30-foot level. On this level, they decided that it was time to head back to the mainland.

There have been many tall-tales told over the years as to who may have dug the famous Oak Island Money Pit. I believe there have been enough books written on this subject that I need not repeat these same old stories.

In 1803, these three young men returned to Oak Island with a crew known as the *Onslow Company*. Before long, these young men and the new crew dug their way back down to another oak log floor on the 30-foot level. This was the level where these three young men had come to a stop eight years earlier. They removed this oak log floor and continued to dig down another 10 feet, where they discovered another oak floor on the 40-foot level. They found that it was covered with boards and a layer of charcoal.

They commenced digging and found an oak log floor on the 50-foot level, and discovered that it was covered with a layer of putty-clay. There was enough putty of such high quality that the people in Mahone Bay region were able to use it as glazing for the windows of more than 20 houses. It was on this level that "small stones" were discovered. It has been claimed that there were "strange symbols" inscribed on each stone. Today nothing has surfaced to reveal what was inscribed on those stones.

On the 60-foot level, another oak floor was discovered, and this one was covered with coconut fibre. This fibre was thought to have come from the Caribbean. Then on the 70-foot level, an oak floor was said to be tiered with putty. Another oak floor was discovered on the 80-foot level.

When they reached the 90-foot level, something very different was waiting for them. It was a flat stone slab weighing 175 pounds. It was said to be about 3 feet long and 1 foot wide. It was only a few inches thick, with a very olive tinge. When this stone was flipped over, it had symbols or characters carved on the side that had been face down. This freestone was different from any stones on the mainland of Nova Scotia. It was covered with strange markings, which included crosses, triangles, dots, squares and circles. Some people claim that these writings were Tifinagh, Berber, Libyan, Tuareg, or Phoenician script.

According to Lionel Fanthorpe, co-author of the book *The Oak Island Mystery* (1994): "Harry Marshall helped to carry the stone out of the shaft said it was not like anything he ever seen in Nova Scotia. In fact, he thought it to be a form of Porphyry Stone." Fanthorpe goes on to mention that "porphyry is not very common, but one can find it in Egypt." (Lionel Fanthrope YouTube video: "Oak Island Mystery History Channel Documentaries.")

It is interesting to me that the writings on this stone were placed face-down. There have been many interpretations as to the message on this stone. At this point, I find no need to repeat what has been deciphered over the years concerning the possible message inscribed on that stone.

When the men of the Onslow Company reached the 90-foot level, Harry Hubbards mentioned in 2008: "When one of the men used a crowbar and probed the remaining soil, he not only struck a hard, impenetrable material but may very well have triggered some sort of booby trap. Possibly jarring one or two oak logs, and at that point they discontinued the dig." (Source: The Illinois Caves)

During that night when they were at home, the pit became filled with water. In the morning when they returned, they discovered that the water filled the pit to the 33-foot level. This would be the sea level that surrounded Oak Island.

In fact, if these men had continued their excavation the previous evening and removed that 90-foot oak log floor, they no doubt would have made it down to the 100-foot level. That would have resulted in their death, as the sea water would have gushed in on them via the Smith Cove tunnel- a 500-foot-long booby trap connection.

Over the years, there has been some confusion as to various discoveries made down in that famous Money Pit. I have decided not to go into all the details regarding what was and was not discovered over the more than 255 years on that island. What I do find very interesting are the *claimed* tunnels, subterranean chambers, and the man-made artificial beach in the Smith's Cove area.

In 1849, the *Truro Company* began digging in the Oak Island Money Pit. At the 100-foot level, they discovered a wood platform by means of using a pot auger. They drilled through 5 inches of a spruce platform, 12 inches of an empty cavity, then 12 inches of oak. After that, their drill bit went through 22 inches of metal in pieces, 8 inches of oak, another 22 inches of metal, 4 inches of oak, and 6 inches of spruce. Below this, they encountered 7 feet of clay. When the auger was brought to the surface, it had only contained "three small links of gold chain." They assumed this to be the treasure chest. They discontinued their drilling at the depth of almost the 110-foot level.

In 1897, the *Oak Island Treasure Company,* after reaching the 90-foot level, commenced drilling a hole through 5 inches of oak. At the 126-foot level, they stuck an iron obstruction which was very solid. After "4 hours of drilling," they only were able to penetrate the metal "1/2 inch" and were able to go no further. Then they drilled 1-foot away from the first hole, and this time they slipped past the obstruction. They also discovered a piece of parchment somewhere between the 126-153-foot levels. It appears to have two letters, written with a quill pen in Indian ink. Some people have claimed it that these letters may be any of the following: "vi, wi, ri."

In what is referred to as the *Becker Hole,* a cavity was found from 202 to 209 feet. Below that was a ½ inch iron plate which the diamond drill could not penetrate. Although the cored disc from the iron plate was not recovered, the identification of the drill bit cutting through solid metal was made. This was based on the unmistakable sound of a diamond drill bit cutting through a solid metal object. However, the hole was "not able to be advanced below the iron plate" and thus it was not possible to determine if it was the cover of an iron-lined vault.

In the early 1970s, the *Triton Alliance Ltd.*, headed by David Tobias of Montreal, along with Dan Blankenship, drilled down 180 feet north east of the Oak Island Money Pit. This exploratory drill hole was named *Borehole 10-X*. They got down to bedrock at 180 feet, and entered a large cavity at the depth of 230 feet. They brought up metal that looked like lead, found in the form of smelted steel.

In August 1971, the *CBC Television of Halifax* lowered a camera down into the water filled cavity. Mr. Blankenship claims to have spotted a "severed human hand" floating in the water. To his delight, the camera focused on what looked like two or three "wooden chests" with distinctively "curved tops." They also spotted what appeared to be an upright handle, pick-axe or hammer, with several man-made timbers which stuck out from the roof of the cavity.

The cavity measured about 20x18 feet and 7-feet in height. They claimed to have located what looked like a partly preserved "human body" slumped against the wall of the flooded cavern. Within the cavern there was strong visual evidence of entrances to two other tunnels or cavities.

An article in the December 7, 1971 issue of the *Halifax Chronicle Herald* mentioned: "A diver had been lowered 235 feet into this chamber or cavern. He could see a `ghostly ceiling' having 8-10 `V' shaped gouges extending upwards in the ceiling. Reflecting of his light on the ceiling in certain spots, the ceiling resembled fluorescent light. He could not see the bottom that he was standing on.

"The shaft and the cavern are now filled with water. This came about after 200 years of people attempting to dig up what they assumed was buried treasure, etc."

A chamber was claimed to have been discovered at least 235-feet down in the shaft. Here is what I believe took place in ancient times: When the ancient miners reached the 170-foot level, they encountered what is known as "anhydrite stone." They continued to dig down through another 60-80 feet of "broken anhydrite." Once they reached the depth of about 235 feet, they began to dig what I would refer to as the "eastern and southern cavern or chambers."

The southern chamber is believed to be about 180-feet long. The length of "eastern cavern/chamber" is unknown. These two tunnels were cut through what is known as the "competent anhydrite" (solid anhydrite). In the "southern tunnel," a chamber was discovered that measured approximately 20x18 feet and 7-feet in height. It is believed that this chamber had 8-10 "V" shaped gouges extending upwards in the ceiling.

*Smith's Cove Tunnel*: The first tunnel was discovered by the *Halifax Company* on the 100-foot level of the Money Pit. An opening to this tunnel stretched 500 feet to Smith's Cove (I have named this the East Tunnel). This tunnel was made with round stones, which had dimension of 2.6-feet in width by 4-feet in height, with an upward gradient of 22.5 degrees. The end of this tunnel, which came out at Smiths Cove, had five well-laid-out openings made up of cobble stones.

No 1: *Smiths Cove Tunnel* had some very interesting claims connected with it over the years. The end of this 500-foot tunnel came out in the beach area of Smith's Cove. Five perfectly formed "box drains" were discovered there, each one approximately eight inches in width, made of flat stones laid along the sides, and across the top, embedded into the beach. Further exploration revealed that the "five drains" extended out along the entire 145-foot area shoreline in a "finger-like fan formation," running back from the ocean and dropping deeper as they approached the shoreline. The drains converged on each other, over a much larger funnel-like central drain just above the high mark.

These drains were covered with materials that go beyond the norm. An article in the newspaper "The Colonist" stated: "Over these came a layer of blue-sand, such as before had not been on the island, and over the sand was spread gravel indigenous to the coast."

Point of interest: When the men were trying to build a coffer-dam for holding the tides back, to keep the ocean water from covering these 5 fingers like drains, they also found out someone else had built another cofferdam in this same area. No doubt this newly discovered cofferdam was constructed by the original builders. It served the same purpose: to keep the water back.

No 2: *Joudrey's Cove Tunnel*: A second tunnel was claimed to have been discovered on the 130-foot level. This tunnel came out in the Joudrey's Cove area. A rough estimation on my part is that tunnel would have been a about 1300-feet long.

No. 3: *South Shore Cove Tunnel*: A third flood tunnel was discovered on the 160-foot level. This tunnel is claimed to have extended out 2000-feet to the South Shore Cove. The size of this tunnel and the gradient are unknown.

# Oak Island Nova Scotia

*Smith's Cove Tunnel*: The first tunnel was discovered by the *Halifax Company* on the 100-foot level of the Money Pit. An opening to this tunnel stretched 500 feet to Smith's Cove. (I have named this the East Tunnel.) This tunnel was made with round stones, which had the dimension of 2.6-feet wide by 4-feet high, with an upward gradient of 22.5 degrees. The end of this tunnel which came out at Smiths Cove had five well laid out openings made up of cobble stones.

No 1: *Smiths Cove Tunnel* had some very interesting claims connected with it over the years. The end of this 500-foot tunnel came out in the beach area of Smith's Cove. What was discovered there were five perfectly formed "box drains," each one approximately eight inches in width, made of flat stones laid along the sides, and across the top, embedded into the beach. Further exploration revealed that the "five drains" extended out along the entire 145-foot area shoreline in a "finger-like fan formation," running back from the ocean and dropping deeper as they approached the shoreline. The drains converged on each other, over a much larger funnel-like central drain just above the high mark.

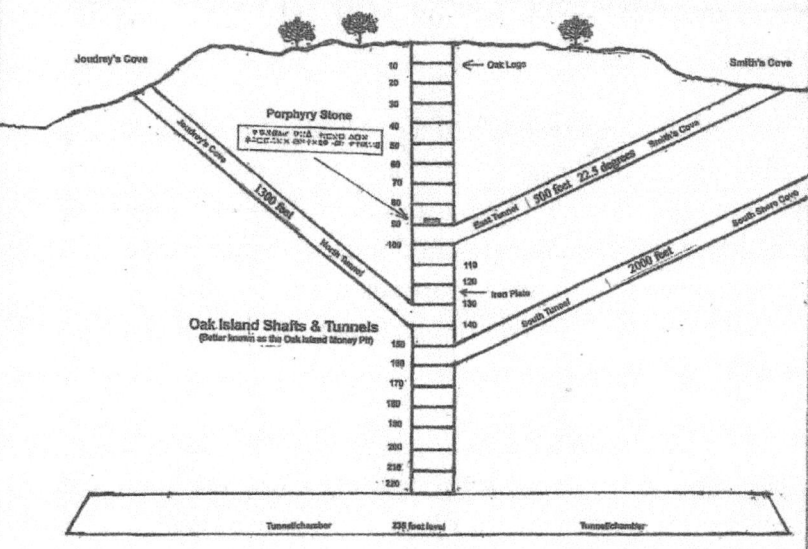

These drains were covered with materials that go beyond the norm. An article in the newspaper "The Colonist" stated: "Over these came a layer of blue-sand, such as before had not been on the island, and over the sand was spread gravel indigenous to the coast."

Point of interest: When the men were trying to build a coffer-dam for holding the tides back, to keep the ocean water from covering these 5 fingers like drains, they also found out someone else had built another coffer dam in this same area. No doubt this newly discovered coffer dam was constructed by the original builders. It served the same purpose to keep the water back.

No 2: *Joudrey's Cove Tunnel*: A second tunnel was claimed to have been discovered on the 130-foot level. This tunnel came out in the Joudrey's Cove area. A rough estimation on my part is that tunnel would have been a about 1300-feet long.

No. 3: *South Shore Cove Tunnel*: A third flood tunnel was discovered on the 160-foot level. This tunnel is claimed to have extended out 2000-feet to the South Shore Cove. The size of this tunnel and the gradient are unknown.

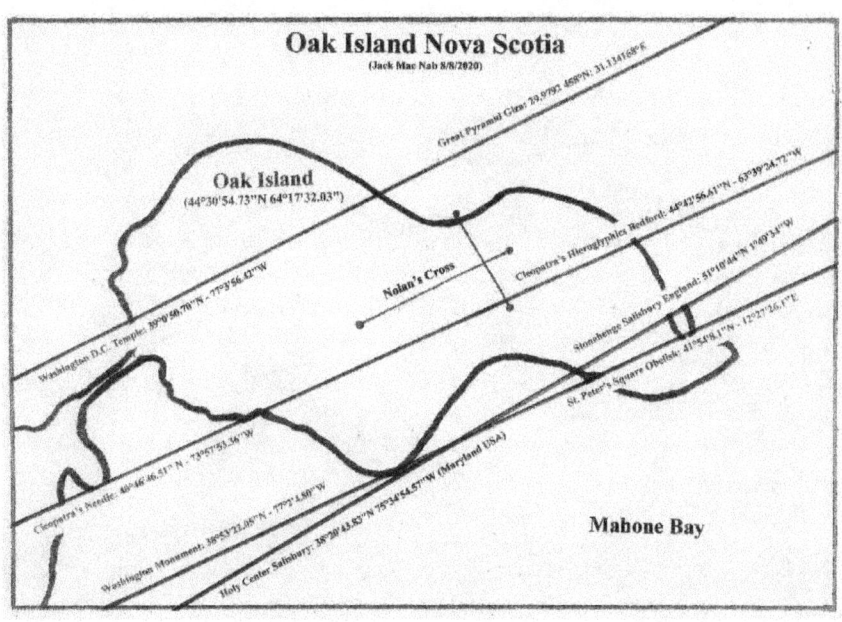

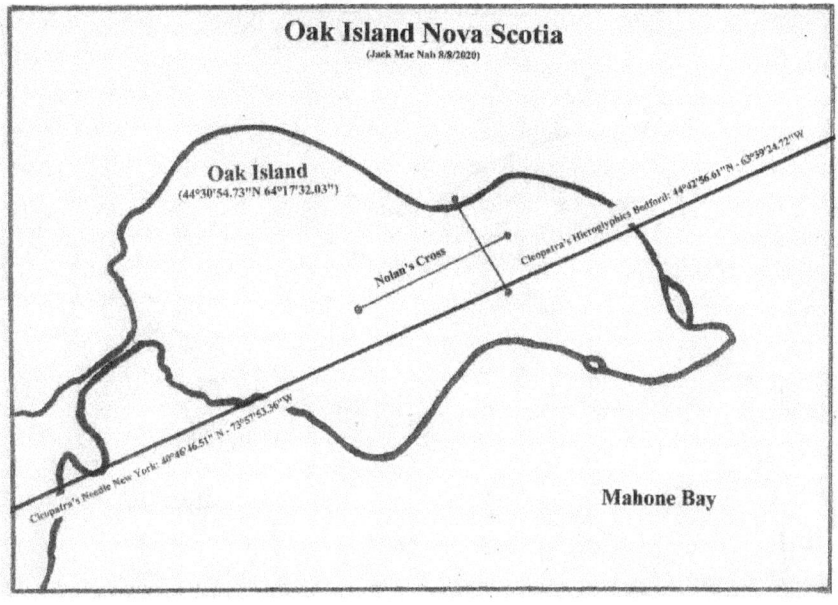

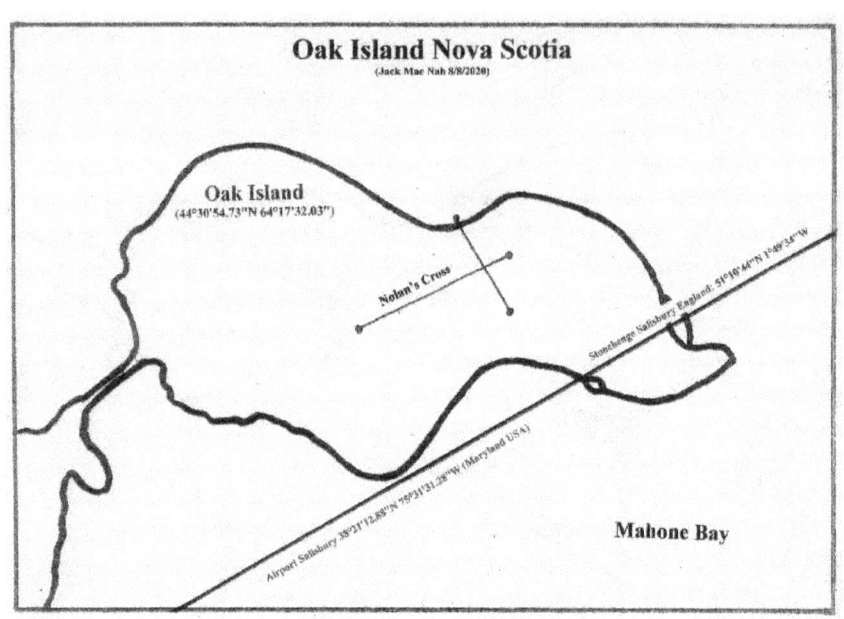

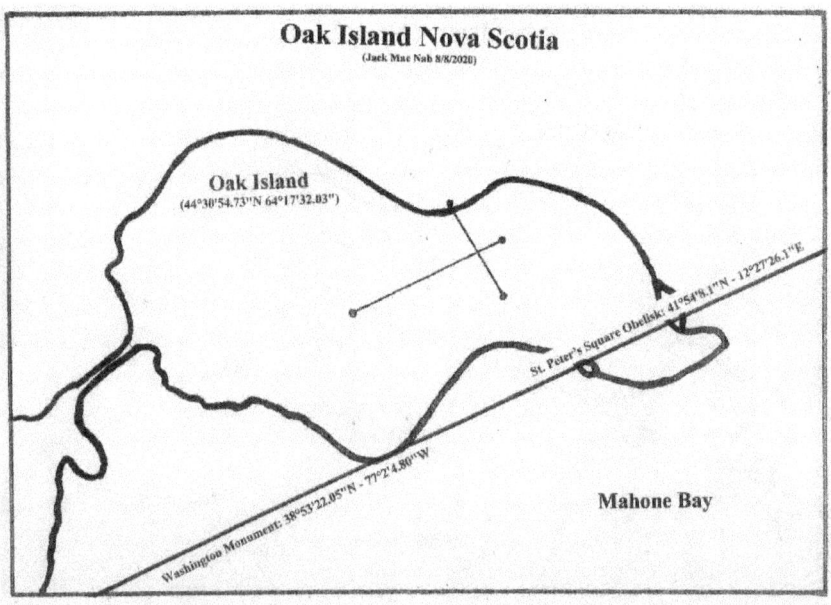

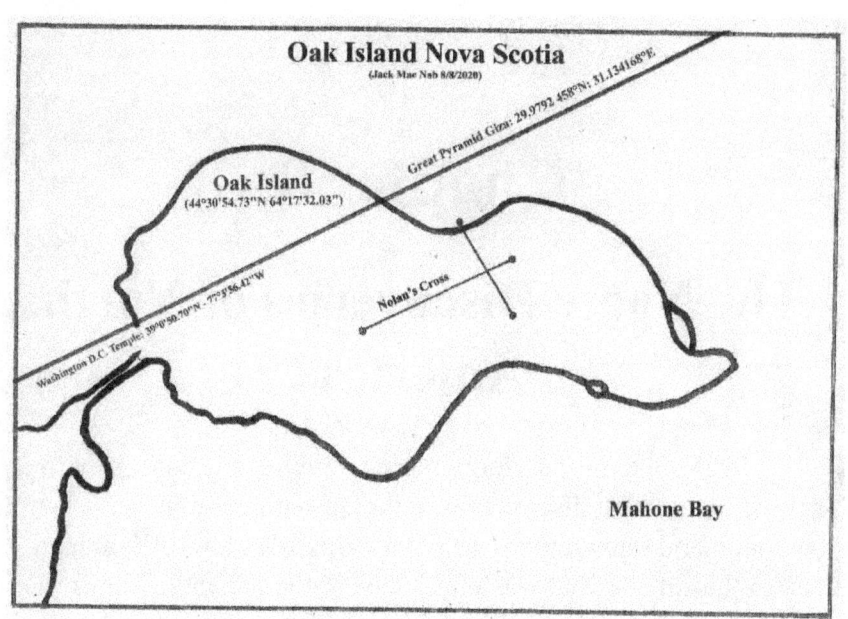

# Chapter 8

# The Norse Discoveries of North America

In 1960, explorer Helge Ingstad and his archeologist wife, Anne Stine Ingstad, discovered the Norse settlement in Newfoundland known today as L'Anse aux Meadows. What lead them to this site is what was mentioned in the Icelandic Sagas known as the Saga of the Greenlanders and the Saga of Erik the Red. With lots of speculation on the part of Helge and Anne, in addition to their being at the right place at the right time, this event changed the history of Canada for all time.

The first time I had heard about the possibility of Vinland being located along Northeast coast of New Brunswick was when I attended a public discourse given by Anne Stine Ingstad in Truro, Nova Scotia (2008). This opened up a whole new view as to what may or may not have taken place during these early Norse voyages to the Maritime Provinces of Canada.

Dr. Birgitta Wallace believes that the location of Hop mentioned in the Norse Sagas is located in the Miramichi-Chaleur Bay area in northeastern New Brunswick. Wallace appears to claim that grapes are not native to either Prince Edward Island or Nova Scotia. Dr. Birgitta Wallace is a senior archaeologist emerita with Parks Canada. Wallace mentions: "Hop may not be the name of just one settlement, but rather an area where the Vikings may have created multiple short-term (seasonal) settlements whose precise locations varied from year to year…etc." (LIVE SCIENCE 3/6/2018 by Qwen Jarus)

It has been speculated that Leif Erikson, in about 1000 A.D., built his "two booths" in the Miramichi-Chaleur Bay area of New Brunswick, "At a place where a river (Restigouche River) flows out of a lake" (Chaleur Bay).

It appears that "Leif's Booths in Vinland" mentioned by Thorvalt Erikson in 1004 A.D., located in the place claimed "Hop Camp", were situated in the Miramichi-Chaleur Bay, New Brunswick. The Icelandic Sagas also referred to the "Leifsbudir" settlement of "two booths" made earlier by Lief Erikson in 1000 A.D.

Following their references to Leif's "two booths", the Sagas describe how Thorvalt Erikson sailed to a place where "there were many islands." This is a bit of a big leap, but I am speculating that these "islands" were located in the Penobscot Harbour area of Maine. I will elaborate on this later.

There are four well known voyages to North America that were recorded in the Norse Sagas. It is my belief that certain Norse voyages made it as far as the South Shore of Nova Scotia. To date, no Norse artifacts have been found in Nova Scotia to prove this claim beyond a reasonable doubt. My claims about the South Shore and Southern Nova Scotia being Vinland should not be viewed as an absolute fact, although I believe they are very plausible.

## Bjarni Herjólfsson voyage to North America - 986 A. D.

Greenlanders Saga 970 - 1030
1st Norse Voyage to North America
(Newfoundland, Labrador, Baffin Island)

Bjarni was born in Iceland and later became a merchant captain in Norway. The following is the 986 A.D., Bjarni

Herjólfsson voyage to America. This Greenlanders Saga does not reveal solid clues as to what part of America he was able to spot. There was no landfall. It is believed that he spotted Newfoundland, Labrador, and Baffin Island, and then returned to Greenland.

Bjarni (Herjólfsson)
Set sail for Greenland
After sailing for 3 days (from Iceland)
A fair wind fell

There arose north winds and fogs
They knew not where they were
And thus, it continued for many days

After that they saw the sun again
And could discover the sky
They now made sail
And sailed for that day
Before they saw land (?)
And counselled with each other about
"What land could this be?"
Bjarne said as he thought:
"Could it not be Greenland?"
They asked:
"Do you wish to sail to this land or not?"
Bjarne said:
"My advice is to set sail close to the land" (?)

So, they did and soon saw land (?)
Without mountains
Covered with wood (Central Labrador Coast)
And had small heights

Then left the land on their starboard side
And let the stern turn from the land (Central Labrador Coast)
Afterwards they sailed two days
Before they saw another land (**Baffin Island**)

They asked Bjarne:
"Was this Greenland?"
But he said: "It is too little to be Greenland."
"Because in Greenland there are very high ice-hills."

They soon approached the land
And saw that it was a flat land
Covered with wood (Baffin Island)
(Then they sailed back to Greenland)

# Leif Erikson Voyage to North America - 1000 A.D.

Greenlanders Saga 970 - 1030
2nd Norse Voyage to North America.
A crew of 35 men
(Maritime Provinces - Central Labrador Coast - Baffin Island)

## PART 1:

Leif Erikson
The son of Erik the Red
Was told about voyage of Bjarni Herjólfsson

That he (Bjarni)
Had seen unknown lands (North America)
People thought he had no curiosity (no interest)
Had nothing to relate about
These countries (Newfoundland - Central Labrador Coast - Baffin Island)

Leif went to Bjarni
Bought a ship off him
And engaged men for it
So that there were 35 men in all

Then went they on board
And after sailing out to sea
Found another land (Helleland: Baffin Island)

## PART 2:

They sailed again to that land (Central Labrador Coast)
Cast anchor, put off boats, went on shore
This land was flat and covered with wood
White sands were far around
Where they went the shore was low
Then, said Lief:
"This land shall be named after its qualities
And called it Markland." (Woodland; Central Labrador Coast)

## PART 3:

They then immediately returned to the ship
Now sailed they thence (away from Labrador)
Into the open sea with a northeast wind.
They were two days at sea (Sailed southward past Newfoundland)
Before they saw land (Nova Scotia).
They sailed thither
And came to an island (Tancock Island)
That lay to the eastward of land.

Went up there looked round them in good weather
Observed that there was dew
Upon the grass and it so happened
That they touched the dew with their hands
And raised the fingers to the mouth.
They thought that they had before
Tasted anything so sweet.

After that they went to the ship
Sailed into a sound
That lay between the island, (?)
And a ness (a headland or promontory)
That ran out to the eastward of the land

And then steered westwards past the ness

## PART 4:

It was a very shallow at the ebb tide
And their ship stood up
So that it was far to see
From the ship to the water

But so much did they desire to land
That they did not give themselves time
To wait until the water rose under the ship
But ran at once to shore
At a place where a river (?)
Flows out of a lake (?)

And there cast anchors
Bought up from the ship
Their skin cots
And made their booths (two booths)

After this they took counsel
And formed the resolution
Of remaining there for the winter
Built their large houses

There was no want of salmon
Either in the river
Or in the lake
Larger salmon than they had before seen

The nature of the country
Was as they though so good that cattle,
Would not require house feeding in winter
For there came no frost in winter
And little did the grass wither

Day and night were more equal
In Greenland or Iceland

For on the shortest day was the sun
Above the horizon
Half-past seven in the afternoon
Till half-past four in the afternoon

## PART 6:

They slept now for the night but in the morning
Leif said to the sailors:
"We will now set about two things
In that the one day we gather grapes" (Blackberries)

And the other day we cut vines and fell trees
Leif said:
"Their longboats filled with grapes
Now cargo cut down for the ship"

## PART 7:

And when spring came
They got ready and sailed away
Leif gave the land a named after its qualities
And called it "Vinland or Wineland." (Southern Nova Scotia)

They (Leif and crew)
Sailed now into the open sea (Atlantic Ocean)
Had a fair wind
Until they saw Greenland

# Thorvalt Erikson Voyage to North America (1004 A.D.)

Greenlanders' Saga
3rd Voyage to North America
(Baffin Island - Central Labrador Coast Nova Scotia)

## Part 1:

Thorvald Eriksson
Made ready for this voyage
With 30 men
Took counsel with Leif Erikson
His brother

Then made their ship ready
And put to sea (Greenland)
Nothing is told of their voyage
Until they came to
Leif's Booths in Vinland (South Shore Nova Scotia)

## PART 2:

There they laid up their ship
Spent a pleasant winter (South Shore NS)
Caught fish for the support
But in the spring

Said Thorvalt:
"That they should make ready the ship
And that some of the men
Should take the longboat
Round the western part of the land
And explore there during the summer."
To them appeared the land
Fair and woody but a short distance
Between the wood and the sea white sand (South Shore NS)
There were many islands (?)
And much shallow water
They found neither dwelling
Nor men nor beast

Except upon an island (not Oak Island)
To the westward (Western Shore Mahone)

Where they found a corn-shed of wood (not Oak Island)
But many works of men they found not
(Oak Island was not an island in and about 1000 - 1100 A.D.)

## PART 3:

They then went back
Came to Leif's booths (South Shore Nova Scotia)
In the autumn

But the next summer
Went Thorvalt eastward (along the Eastern Shore of Nova Scotia)
With the ship round the land (rounded Cape Canso)
To the northward hence came a heavy storm

Upon them went then off a ness (Cape Canso)
So that they were driven on shore
The keel broke off the ship
They remained here a long time
And repaired the ship

Then said Thorvalt to his companions:
"Now will I that we fix the keel upon the ness
and call it Keelness?" (Kjalarness; Cape Canso NS)
And so, they did after that they sailed away around (round Cape Canso)
The eastern shores of the land (southward along the Eastern Shore NS)

## PART 4:

And into the mouths of the firths that lay nearest there (?)
To a point of land which stretched out
Was covered all over with wood
There they came to with the ship
Shoved out a plank to the land
And Thorvalt went up to the country
With all his companions

He then said:
"Here it is beautiful, here would I like
To raise my dwelling." (South Shore of Nova Scotia)
Then went to the ship
Saw the sand within the promontory
Three elevations
Saw there three shin boats (canoes)
Three men under each

## PART 5:

A skirmish took place.
Eight natives killed
Thorvalt stuck by arrow under the arm
It was a mortal wound

Thorvalt said:
"Bear me at the cape (Cape Canso NS)
There shall ye bury me set up crosses
At my head and feet and call the Krossaness
Forever and all time to come."

Now Thorvald died
They did all they were told to do
And returned to their companions
Dwelt there for the winter (South Shore NS)

Gathered grapes and vines (Wild Blackberries)
For the ship in the spring
Made sail ready for Greenland
Came with their ship in Eriksfjord (Greenland)
Could now tell great tidings to Leif.

# Thorfinn Karlsefni Voyage to North America - 1009 A.D.

Greenlanders Saga 970 - 1030
2nd Norse Voyage to North America.
Crew 60 men & 5 women
Snorri first child in America. (Parents: Karlsefni & Gudrid)
(Baffin Island - Central Labrador Coast - Nova Scotia)

    Thorfinn Karlsefni Norse Voyage to Vinland (1009 A.D.) According to the Saga of Erik the Red, "Straumfjord" was a "fjord" located somewhere in Vinland the Good. For unknown reasons, the name "Straumfjord" (Stream-Isle) is not mentioned in what is known as the Greenlander Saga. It is believed that Thorfinn Karlsefni had established a settlement in the general area of "Straumfjord" in about 1000 years ago. The location of this settlement was referred to in the Norse Sagas as "Hop."

    Dr. Birgiton Wallace, senior archaeologist emerita of Parks Canada, believes that "Hop may not be the name of just one settlement, but rather an area where the Vikings may have created multiple short-term (seasonal) settlements whose precise locations varied from year to year." (LIVE SCIENCE 3/6/2018)

    It is believed that Thorfinn Karlsefni established a settlement "Straumfjord" and named it "Hop." At the Mouth of the Straumfjord there was an Island named the "Straumsey" (Current-isle). The location of this "island" and "fjord" has been highly debated for a very long time.

    The identity the "Straumfjord" is dependent upon where the "Straums-ey Island" was located in Vinland. It has been suggested that Straumfjord is "south" of Hop.

(Wikipedia: "There is no popular or scholarly agreement on the exact location of the Wonderstrands, and Fridtjof

Nansen and Helge Ingstad held that the Saga of Erik the Red in general could not be trusted.")

## PART 1:

According to the Saga of Erik the Red, Thorfinn's longships pulled away from the shores of "Markland" (Labrador) and after sailing for another "two half-days" of sailing (southwards)
They saw land (Nova Scotia)
And sailed under it
There was a cape (Cape Canso Guysborough County NS)
To which they came

They went to the land in boats
And found the keel of a ship
And called the place Kjalarnes [Keelness] (Cape Canso NS)

They cruised along the land (Eastern Shore NS)
Leaving it on the starboard side

## PART 2:

There was a harbourless coast-land
And long sandy strands (South Shore NS)
(Note: "harbourless coast-land" possibly an exaggeration)

They gave also name to the strands (South Shore NS)
Calling them Furdustrandir [wonder-shore]
Because it was tedious to sail by them
Then the coast became indented with creeks
And they directed their ships along the creeks

(Mac Nab: There have been many suggestions made over the year as to the location of "Wonderstrands." I am personally inclined to believe that the stretch of land known as the South Shore, with its many sandy-beaches, appears to fit like a glove. The South Shore is concentrated in the towns of Lunenburg, Chester, Mahone

Bay, Liverpool, the five beaches surrounding Riverport, and the fishing community of Peggy's Cove.)

## PART 3:

They said to Karlsefni that they considered
They had found good and choice land
Then they received them (The Scotch: Haki & Haekja)
 Into their ship (longboat)

And proceeded on their journey
To where the shore was cut into by a firth (small inlets of water)

They directed the ships within the firth (inlet)
There was an island (Straumsey Island)
Lying out in front of the firth
And there were great currents around the island
Which they called Straumsey (Current Isle)
And carried their cargo ashore from the ships
And there they prepared to stay
They had with them cattle of all kinds
And for themselves they sought out
The produce of the land thereabout
There were mountains (hills)
The place was fair to look upon

They gave no heed to anything
Except to explore the land
And they found large pastures

They remained there during the winter
That happened to be a hard one
With no work doing
And they were badly off for food
And the fishing failed

## PART 4:

They (Thorfinn Karlsefni and crew)
Gave also name to the strands
Calling them Furdustrandir (wonder-shore)
(Wonderstrands: South Shore NS)
Because it was tedious to sail by them
Then the coast became indented with creeks
And they directed their ships along the creeks

Two Scotch people,
The man called Haki
And the woman called Haekja

When they had sailed by
The Furdustrandir (South Shore NS)
They put the Scotch people on land

And requested them to run
Into the southern regions (Southern NS)
Seek for choice land
And come back after three half-days were passed

Then did they cast anchors from the ships
And lay there to wait for them
When three days were expired
The Scotch people leapt down from the land
One of them had in his hand a bunch of grapes (Blackberries)
And the other an ear of wild wheat (Fodder or Wild Rice)

## PART 5:

Then they went out to the island (?)
Hoping that something might be got there
From fishing or from what was drifted ashore
In that spot there was little to be got for food
But their cattle found good sustenance

After that they called upon God
Praying that He
Would send them some little store of meat
But their prayer was not so soon granted
As they were eager that it should be

Thorhall disappeared from sight
And they went to seek him
And sought for three half-days continuously

On the fourth half-day Karlsefni and Bjarni
Found him on the peak of a crag
He lay with his face to the sky
With both eyes and mouth and nostrils wide open
Clawing and pinching himself
And reciting something

They asked why he had come there
He replied that it was of no importance
Begged them not to wonder there-at
For himself he had lived so long
They needed not to take any account of him
They begged him to go home with them
And he did so

## PART 6:

Then was granted to them opportunity of fishing
After that there was no lack of food that spring
They went back again from the island (?)
Within Straumsfjord (?)

And obtained food from both sides
From hunting on the mainland
From gathering eggs
And from fishing on the side of the sea

## PART 7:

When summer was at hand
They discussed about their journey
And made an arrangement
Thorhall the Sportsman
Wished to proceed northwards (They did not sail northward as suggested)
Along Furdustrandir (Wonderstand) (South Shore NS)

And off Kjalarnes (Cape Canso NS)
And so, seek Vinland (South Shore NS)

But Karlsefni desired to proceed southwards
Along the land and away from the east (They did not sail southwards as suggested)

Because the land appeared to him
The better the further south he went (They now sailed southward)
And he thought it also more advisable
To explore in both directions

Then did Thorhall make ready
For his journey out by the islands (?)
And there volunteered for the expedition
With him not more than nine men
But with Karlsefni there went (?)
The remainder of the company

One day when Thorhall was carrying water
To his ship he drank and recited this verse:
"The clashers of weapons did say,
When I came here,
 That I should have the best of drink,
Eager God of the war-helmet!
(Though it becomes me not to complain,
Before the common people)
I am made to raise the bucket;
Wine has not moistened my beard,

Rather do I kneel at the fountain."

Afterwards they put to sea,
And Karlsefni accompanied them by the island (?)
Before they hoisted sail Thorhall recited a verse:
"Go we back where our countrymen are,
Let us make the skilled hawk of the sand-heaven,
Explore the broad ship-courses;
While the dauntless rousers of the sword-storm,
Who praise the land (South Shore NS)
And cook whale, dwell on Furdustrandir. (Wonderstrand)

## PART 8:

Then they left, and sailed northwards
(Thorvalt sailed back to Ireland where he died)
Along Furdustrandir (Wonderstrand: South Shore Nova Scotia)
And Kjalarnes (Cape Canso NS)
And attempted there to sail
Against a wind from the west

A gale came upon them
And drove them onwards against Ireland (Shipwrecked in Ireland)
And there were they severely treated
And thralled and beaten. (subject to being enslaved)
Then Thorhall lost his life (died in Ireland)

## PART 9:

Karlsefni proceeded southwards
Along the land (along the South Shore)
With Snorri and Freydis
And the rest of the company

They journeyed took a long while
Until they arrived at a river (?)
That came down from the land (Nova Scotia)
And fell into a lake (?)
And so on to the sea (Atlantic Ocean)

There were large islands (?)
Off the mouth of the river
And they could not come into the river
Except at high flood-tide

Karlsefni and his people sailed
To the mouth of the river
And called the land Hop

## PART 10:

There they found fields of wild wheat (Fodder or Wild Rice)
Wherever there were low grounds
And the vine in all places (Blackberry Bushes)

Where there was rough rising ground
Every rivulet
There was full of fish
They made holes (Fish Weirs)
Where the land and water joined
Where the tide went highest
And when it ebbed
They found halibut in the holes

## PART 11:

There were a great plenty of wild animals
Of every form in the wood
They were there half a month
Amusing themselves
And not becoming aware of anything

Their cattle they had with them
Early one morning as they looked around
They beheld nine canoes made of hide
And snout-like staves
Were, being brandished from the boats
They made a noise like flails

And twisted round in the direction of the sun's motion

Then Karlsefni said:
"What will this betoken?"
Snorri answered him:
"It may be that it is a token of peace;
Let us take a white shield and go to meet them."

And so, they did.
Then did they in the canoes row forwards
And showed surprise at them
And came to land

They were short men, ill-looking
With their hair in disorderly fashion on their heads
They were large-eyed, and had broad cheeks
And they stayed there awhile in astonishment
Afterwards they rowed away to the south
Off the headland

## PART 12:

They had built their settlements
Up above the lake
Some of the dwellings
Were well within the land
But some were near the lake (?)

Now they remained there that winter
They had no snow (meaning not as much snow like in Greenland)
Whatever and all their cattle
Went out to graze without keepers

## PART 13:

Karlsefni and his company were now of the opinion
That though the land might be choice and good
There would be always war and terror overhanging them
From those who dwelt there before them

They made ready therefore to move away
With intent to go to their own land (South Shore NS)

They sailed forth northwards (along the South Shore)
And found five Skrælingar in jackets of skin
Sleeping near the sea
And they had with them a chest
And in it was marrow of animals mixed with blood
And they considered that these must have been outlawed
They slew them

Afterwards they came to a headland (?)
And a multitude of wild animals
This headland appeared as if it might
Be a cake of cow-dung
Because the animals passed the winter there

## PART 14:

Now they came to Straumsfjord (?)
Where also they had abundance of all kinds
It is said by some that
Bjarni and Freydis remained there
And had 100 men with them
And went no further away

But Karlsefni and Snorri journeyed southwards
Forty men with them
After staying no longer than scarcely
Two months at Hop (?)
Had come back the same summer

Karlsefni set out with a single ship
To seek Thorhall
But the rest of the company
Remained behind

He and his people
Went northwards off Kjalarnes (Cape Canso NS)

And were then borne onwards towards the west
And the land lay on their larboard-side
And was nothing but wilderness

And when they had proceeded for a long time
There was a river
That came down from the land
Flowing from the east towards the west
They directed their course within the river's mouth
And lay opposite the southern bank

Then they journeyed
Away back again northwards
And saw as they thought
The land of the One-footers

They wished, however
No longer to risk their company
They conjectured the mountains
To be all one range

## PART 15:

Those that is which were at Hop (?)
And those which they now discovered
Almost answering to one another
And it was the same distance
To them on both sides from Straumsfjord (?)

They journeyed back
And were in Straumsfjord (?)
The third winter (3 years)
Then fell the men greatly into backsliding
They who were wifeless pressed
Their claims at the hands of those who were married

Snorri **Thorfinnsson** was born the first autumn
And he was three winters old
Thorfinn Karlsefni's son

When they began their journey home

Now when they sailed from Vinland (South Shore Nova Scotia)
They had a southern wind
And reached Markland (Baffin Island)
Then came they to Greenland
And remained with Erik the Red during the winter.

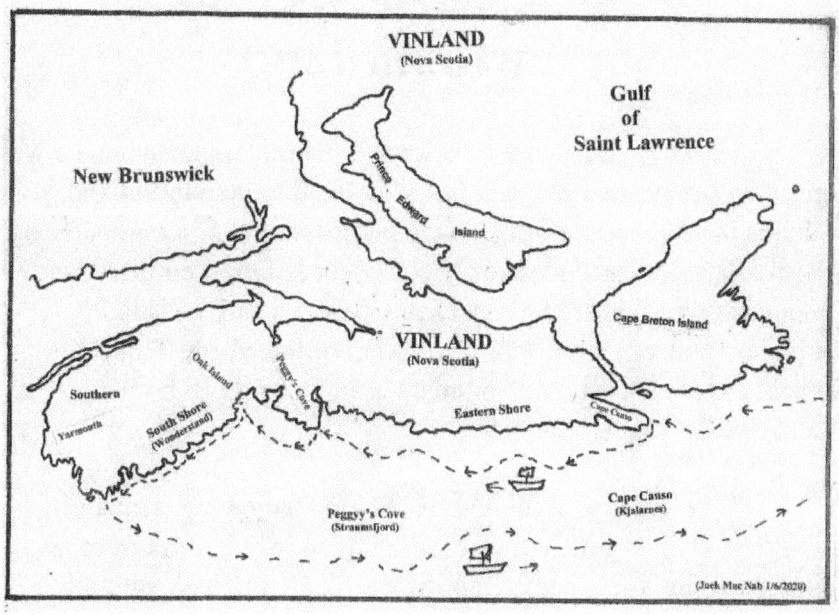

# Chapter 9

# The 1399 Zeno Voyage to Newfoundland

Sir Antonio Zeno wrote down what took place when he was on a ship that made a voyage from Scotland to Newfoundland Canada in 1399. His writings were published in 1558 in Venice by Nicolo Zeno, a descendant of Nicolo Zeno, of the Zeno Brothers. Today his writings are known as the Zeno Narrative. This publication also includes the Zeno Map of the North. This map appears to depict various land masses and islands on both sides of the Atlantic Ocean.

"The younger Zeno published the map, along with a series of letters, claiming he had discovered them in a storeroom in his family's home in Venice. According to Zeno, the map and letters date from around the year 1400 and purportedly describe a long voyage made by the Zeno brothers in the 1390's under the direction of a prince named Zichmni. The voyage supposedly traversed the North Atlantic and, according to some interpretations, reached North America." (Wikipedia)

Most of the following claims about Antonio Zeno's 1399 voyage to the shores of Newfoundland are based on my own research. As mentioned in the Zeno Narrative, the commander of this ship or ships was Prince Zichmni (Zichmini or Zichermni). At this point in time, I am not in a position to speculate as to who this person was or was not. The identity of Zichmni will be classified in my writings as "unknown."

The name of Henry Sinclair does not appear in the Zeno Narrative. To my knowledge, there are no known authentic documents that mention that Sinclair made a voyage of discovery to the New World. Yet it is very possible that he made that voyage, seeing that this suggestion has been connected with that voyage for a very long time.

The Zeno brothers, namely Nicolo (c. 1326–c. 1402) and Antonio Zeno (died c. 1403) were Italian noblemen from Venice who lived in the second half of the 14th century, and who were famous during the Renaissance for a possible but controversial exploration of the North Atlantic and Arctic waters. They were brothers of the Venetian naval hero Carlo Zeno. The Zeno family was an established part of the aristocracy of Venice and held the franchise for transportation between Venice and the Holy Land during the Crusades. *Zeno* is the Italianization of the Venetian surname *Zen*. (Wikipedia)

## New World Issue

For many years, it has been proclaimed that Prince Henry Sinclair made landfall on the soil of Nova Scotia during the month of *"June"* of 1398 AD. Based on new findings, it is believed that Sinclair was engaged in a battle in Scotland in 1398. Assuming that he was in Scotland in 1398, as accepted history contends, it would not be reasonable to conclude that he was in Nova Scotia during that same year. This leads me to believe that this claimed voyage by Sinclair to the New World would have taken place during the following year of 1399. Sinclair could not have made landfall during the month of *"June"*, as the Zeno Narrative clearly mentions this ship or fleet of ships departed during the *"1st of July."* The mention of the month of *"June"* could possibly be a reference to an earlier voyage or later voyage to the New World.

Based on new evidence, Prince Henry Sinclair could not have been Prince Zichmni. When Sinclair was living in Scotland, he was never at any time referred to as a *"prince."* He was only known as an earl or jarl. From this point forward, I will be referring to Sinclair as Earl Henry Sinclair (1345-1403).

It is my belief that Earl Henry Sinclair did not sail as far as Nova Scotia in 1399. Yet, it appears that was on one of those ships along with Sir Antonio Zeno and Prince Zichmni. The Zeno Narrative indicates to me that he did make a voyage of discovery to the New World. He and the Zeno brothers sailed as far as Newfoundland and returned to Scotland during that same year.

The Zeno Narrative mentions: *"Such is the tenor of the letter to which I* (Nicolo Zeno 1326-1402) *have set out here in detail in order to throw light upon another voyage, which was made by Sir Antonio* (Antonio Zeno was a navigator from Venice died in 1403). *He set sail with a considerable number of vessels and men, but had not the chief in command, as he had expected to have. For Zichmni* (unknown) *went in his own person; and I* (Nicolo Zeno the junior) *have a letter* (Zeno Narrative) *describing that enterprise which is to the following effect:*

*Our great preparations for the voyage to Estotiland* (New World) *were begun in an unlucky hour, for exactly three days before our departure, our fisherman died who was to be have been our guide; nevertheless Zichmni* (unknown) *would not give up the enterprise, but in instead of the deceased fishermen, he took some sailors that had come out with him from the island"* (Orkney Islands).

*"Steering westwards, we discovered some islands subject to Frislanda* (Faroe Islands) *and passing by certain shoals, came to Ledovo,* (Lille Dimun Island in the Faroes) *where we stayed seven days to refresh ourselves and to furnish the fleet with necessaries."* (The men let down anchors on the 26th of June somewhere along the coastline of Lille Dimon Island)

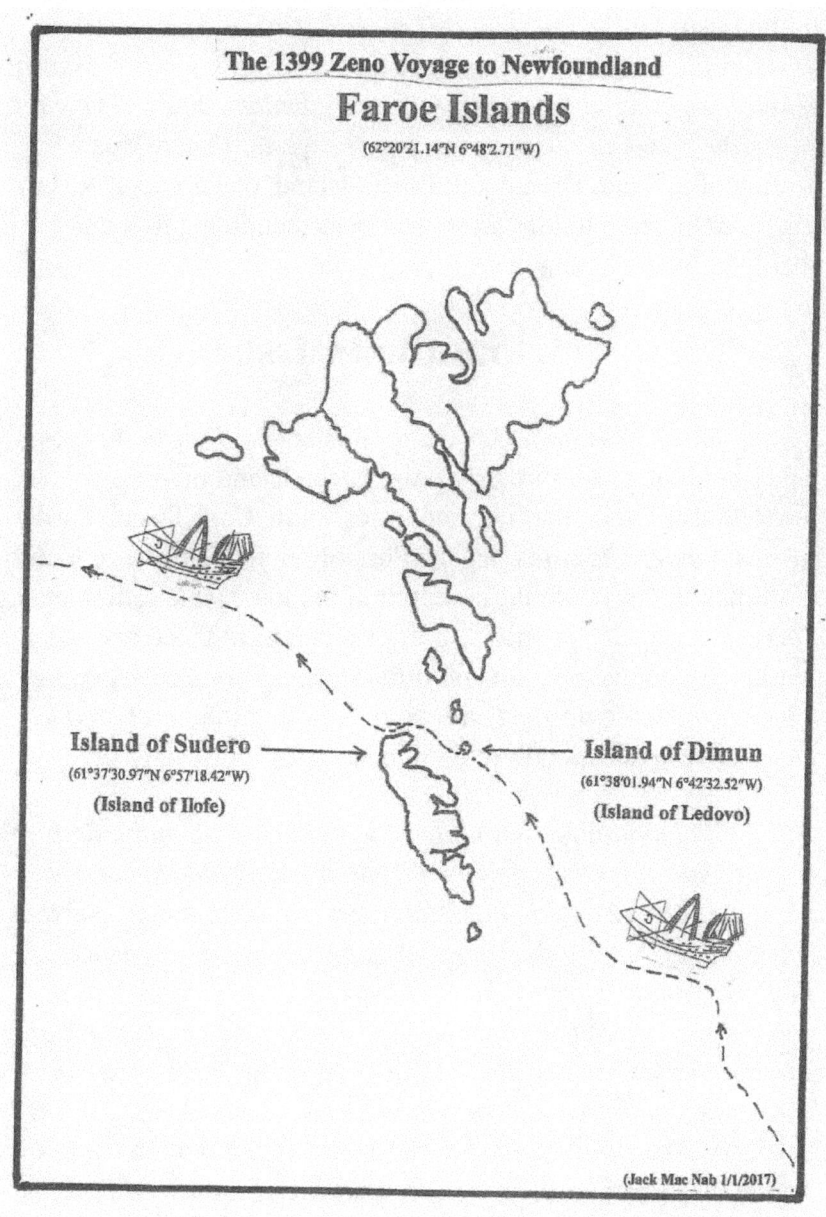

"*Departing thence* (From Lille Dimun Island in the Faroes) *we arrived on the first of July* (1399) *at the Island of Ilofe;* (Sudero Island in the Faroes) *and as the wind was full of our favour, we pushed on;* (They pulled away from Sudero on that same day of July 1,1399) *but not long after, when we were on the open sea, there arose such as great a storm that for eight days we were*

*continuously kept in toil, and driven we knew not where, and a considerable number of boats were lost. At length, when the storm abated, we gathered together the scattered boats, and sailed with a prosperous wind, to discover land on the west."* (There was no mention of Iceland, Greenland, Baffin Island, or Labrador. It is my belief that the land to the *"west"* that was mentioned was none other than Newfoundland.)

## Newfoundland Issue

*"Steering strait for it* (Quirpon Island with its two capes, Cape Bauld the most northerly point of the Island of Newfoundland; the other not two miles south, Cape Degrat), *we reached a quiet and safe harbor,* (Possibly Spillar's Cove or Noddy Bay. Sinclair was no doubt in search of the lost Norse settlement at L'Anse aus Meadows, only a short distance from those two bays mentioned) *in which we saw an infinite number of armed people, who came running furiously down to the water side, prepared to defend the island"* (Island of Newfoundland).

*"Zichmni* (unknown) *now caused his men to make signs of peace to them, and they sent ten men to us who could speak ten languages, but we could understand none of them, except one that came from the Shetland...They therefore requested our prince* (unknown) *made no reply, beyond inquiring where there was a good harbor, and making signs he intended to depart. Accordingly sailing round about this island* (Quirpon Island), *he put with all his fleet in full sail, into a harbor which he found on the eastern side.* (This *"good harbor"* appears to be Hare Bay, located on the east coast of the Great Northern Peninsula of Newfoundland. There is an island in this bay named Hare Bay Island. This bay should not be confused with the other Hare Bay located further down the east coast near Bonavista Bay)

*"The sailors went on shore to take in wood and water, which they did as quickly as they could, for fear they might be attacked by the islanders; and not without reason, for the inhabitants made signals to their neighbors with fire and smoke, and taking to their arms, the others coming to their aid, they all came running down to the seaside upon our men with bows and arrows, so that many were slain and several wounded. Although we made signs of peace to them, it was of no use, for their rage increased more and more, as though they were fighting for their very existence.*

*Being compelled to depart, we sailed along in a great circuit about the island, being always followed on the hill tops and along the seacoasts by an infinite number of armed men. At length, while doubling the northern cape* (Cape Bauld) *of the island* (Sailing *"round"* Quirpon Island for the second time, then continued sailing past Cape Norman, and then down the Strait of Belle Isle), *we came to upon many shoals, among which we were for ten days in continual danger of losing our whole fleet, but fortunately the weather was very fine* (These *"ten days"* involved sailing *"round"* Cape Ray and into the Gulf of Saint Lawrence and next the Cabot Strait a body of water located between Nova Scotia and Newfoundland.). *All the way till we came to the east cape,* (Cape Race) *we saw the inhabitants still on the hill tops and by the sea coast, keeping with us, howling and shooting at us from a distance to show their animosity toward us. We therefore resolved to put into some safe harbor* (Possibly Placentia Bay or St. Mary's Bay), *and see if we might once again speak with the Shetlander, but we failed in our object; for the people, more like beast than men, stood constantly prepared to beat us back if we should attempt to come on land* (There is no mention of an official landfall being made on the soil of Newfoundland. Yet, some of the men did set foot on the soil in the Hare Bay area for only a very short period of time to gather *"wood and water."*).

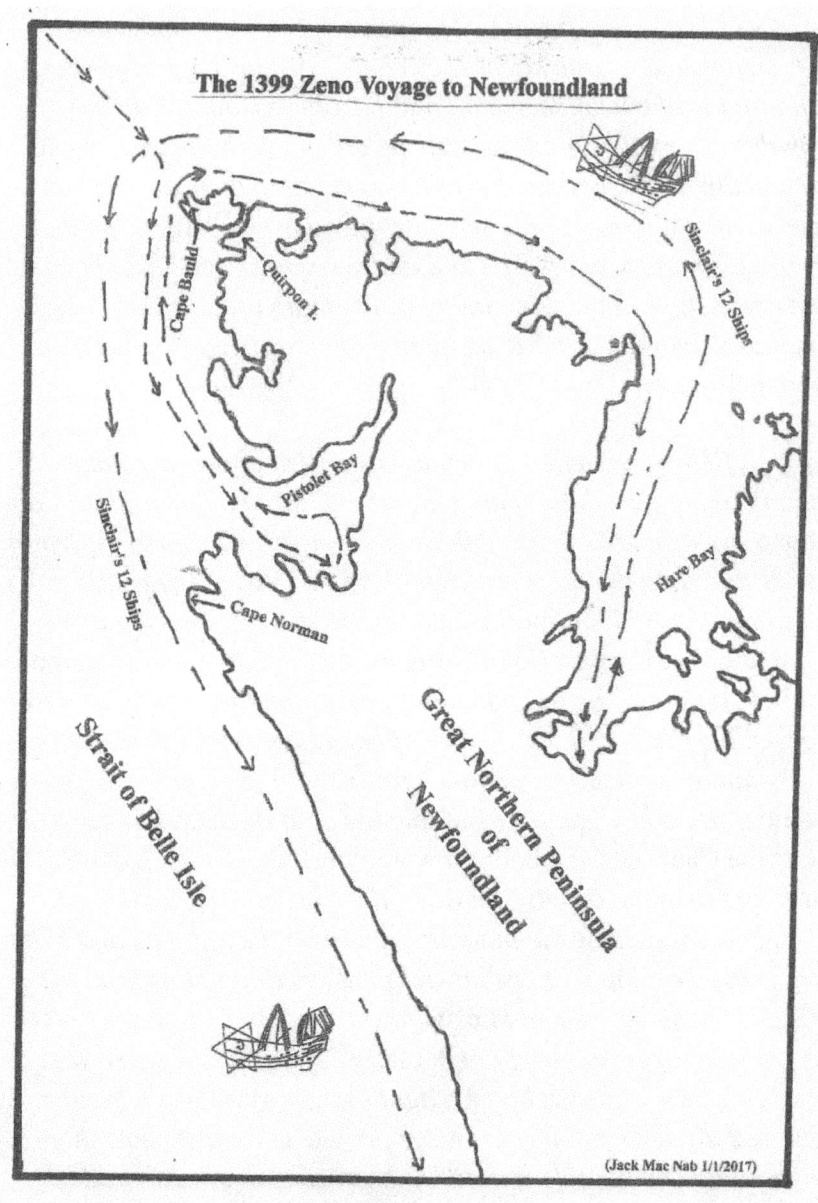

*Wherefore Zichmni* (unknown), *seeing that he could do nothing, and that if he were to persevere in his attempt; the fleet would fall short of provisions* (It is understandable why those in command of this fleet reasoned along these lines. The last time they restocked food supplies was on Lille Dimun Island (*Ledovo*)

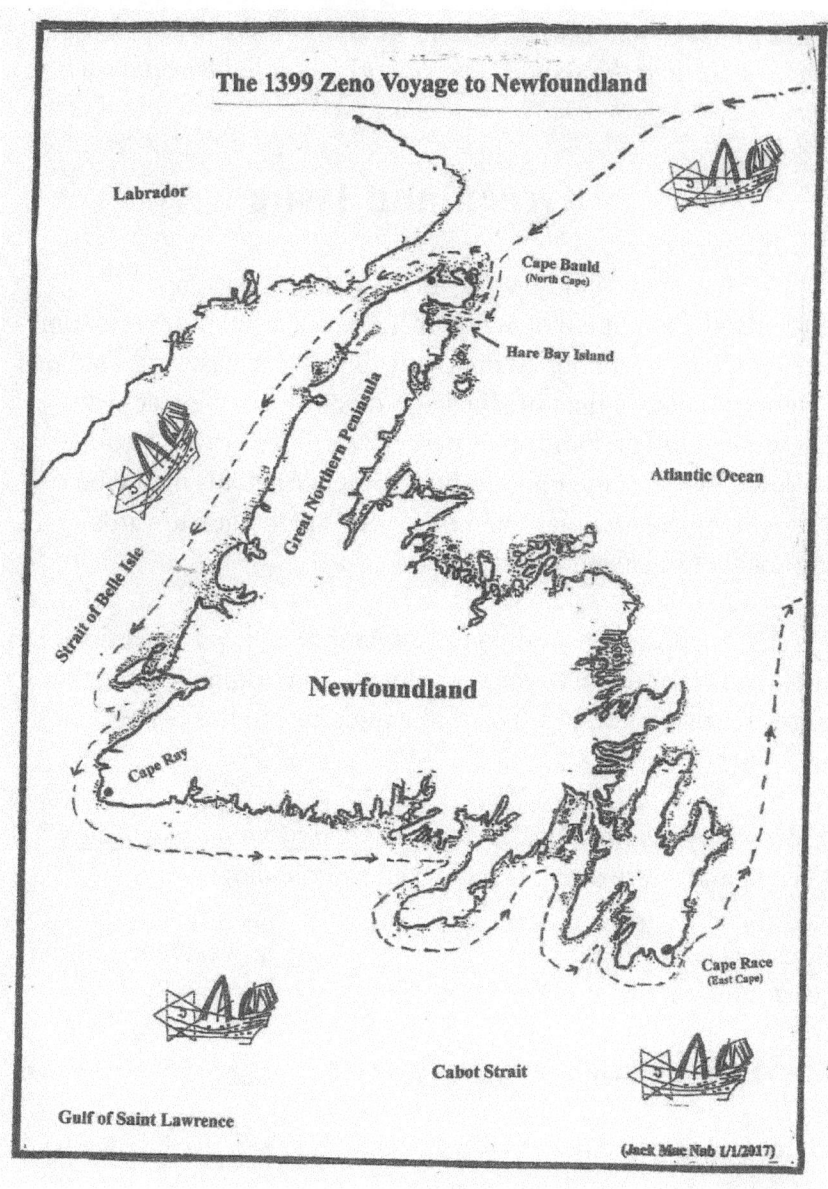

in the Faroe Islands. The next opportunity to do so was in the Hare Bay area of Newfoundland. They went on land for only a very short period of time and were only able to collect some *"wood and water"* but no food supplies. We are looking at a period of more than 18 days since they last stocked up on food on Lille Dimun Island), *took his* (Zichmni) *departure with a fair wind and sailed six days to the westwards; but the wind afterwards shifted to the south-west, and the sea became rough, we sailed four days with the wind aft, at length discovering land...etc."*

## Greenland Issue

To understand how this fleet of ships ended up in Greenland and not Nova Scotia in 1399, we need to review some new findings by author Andrea di Robilant. He has suggested that "Henry Sinclair's fleet of ships could possibly have reached Newfoundland or some other part of North America." He also believes that at some point in time, Sinclair and his men where *"repelled by the natives"* and then they sailed back towards "probably Greenland."

According to Andrea di Robilant, the *"wind"* mentioned in the Zeno Narrative was misinterpreted. The original writing of Zeno Narrative does, in fact, make reference to the *"wind'"* as follows:

1: *So, he took a fair wind and sailed six days to the westwards* (Venetian: *"westwards"* is translated as Ponente)

2: *but when the wind shifted to the South-west* (Venetian: *"South-west"* in Venetian it is known as "Garbin or Garbino.")

3: *and the sea became rough we sailed four days with the wind aft.*

(It took about 10 days of sailing time to reach to reach Greenland after departure from Newfoundland.)

Andrea mentions: "It has been said, on the other hand, that they sailed and then the *'wind shifted to the South-west'*, which would be in the direction of Nova Scotia and New England when sailing down from Newfoundland. I think, however, that this conclusion is based on an error of translation mistake, when

Richard Hakluyt, the Great British geographer, when translating the text of the Zeno narrative to English for the first time, made a fatal mistake with the specific word he mistranslated, namely the name of a `South-west' wind which in Venetian is called Garbino. Andrea claims that Garbino is a `wind' that comes up `from the South-west' towards the North-east, and not the other way around. And my fear is this simple translation caused a lot of confusion, and has contributed to the conclusion that the Zeno Brothers, together with Henry Sinclair, established a colony in North America. I do want to emphasize that the Zeno voyage cannot be used as a base that there was a British/Venetian colony established in North America."

As suggested by Andrea "it appears that Sinclair's 12 ships reached Greenland." He does not give any details as to where Sinclair's fleet of ships where located when this *"wind that came up from-the-South-west."* Andrea appears to support the concept that Sinclair's fleet ships where in the vicinity Newfoundland, Canada. It was then that those 12 ships where pushed northwards by the Garbino `wind' to Greenland. (YouTube video: Andrea_di_Robilant-3)

It was at this point in time that Sinclair's 12 ships sailed out past Cape Race (*east-cape*) Newfoundland, and then were caught in this Garbino *"wind"* that was coming up the *"from South-west."*

It was this *"South-west wind"* that pushed Sinclair's fleet of ships to sail to the North-east, and not to the *"South-west"* as has been claimed by many book writers. This means that Earl Henry Sinclair did not make a voyage of discovery in 1398 to the shores of Nova Scotia, nor did he make a similar voyage in 1399.

When Sinclair's fleet of ships were near Cape Race, Newfoundland, there was only a sailing distance of about 330 miles to reach Nova Scotia. When that fleet of ships was earlier rounding Cape Ra, it was only another 67 miles' sailing distance to reach Cape Breton Island, Nova Scotia. If they had not got caught in that *"wind"* (Garbino) offshore from Cape Race, it is reasonable for me to conclude that they would have continued their voyage until they reached Nova Scotia, their final destination.

## Greenland or Iceland and maybe *not* Nova Scotia!

The Zeno Narrative continues as follows: *"as the sea ran high, we did not know what country it was, we were afraid at first to approach it, but by God's blessing, the wind lulled, and then there came on a great calm. Some of the crew then pulled ashore, and soon returned to our great joy with news that they had found an excellent country and still a better harbor. Upon this we brought our barks and our boats to land, and on entering an excellent harbor, we saw in the distance a great mountain that poured forth smoke, which gave us hope that we should find some inhabitants in the island; neither would Zichmni* (unknown) *rest; although it was a great way off, without sending a hundred soldiers to explore the country, and bring an account of what sort of people the inhabitants were. Meanwhile, they took in a store of wood and water, and caught a considerable quantity of fish and sea-fowl.*

*They also found an abundance of birds' eggs, that our men, who were half famished, ate of them to repletion. While we were at anchor here, the month of June came in, and the air in the island was mild and that this pleasant place was uninhabited. To the harbor we gave the name Trin, and the headland which stretched out into the sea we called Cape de Trin. After eight days the hundred soldiers returned, and brought word that they had been through the island and up to the mountain, and that the smoke was a natural thing proceeding from a great fire in the bottom of the hill, which issued a certain matter like pitch, which ran into the sea, and that thereabouts dwelt a great multitudes of people, half wild, and living in caves. They were small in structure, and very timid; for as soon as they saw our people they fled into their holes. They reported also that there was a large river, and a very good and safe harbor. When Zichmni* (unknown) *heard this, and noticed that the place had a wholesome and pure atmosphere, a fertile soil, good rivers, and so many other conveniences, he conceived the idea of fixing his abode there, and founding a city.*

*But his people, having passed through a voyage so full of fatigues, began to murmur, and to say that they wished to return to their homes, for that winter was not far off, and if they allowed it once to act in, they would not be able to get away before the following summer. He therefore retained only the row boats and such of the people as were willing to stay with him, and send all the rest away in the ships, appointing me* (Antonio Zeno), *against my will, to be their captain.*

*"Having no choice, therefore, I departed, and sailed twenty days to the eastwards without sight of any land; then, turning my course towards the south-east, in five days I lighted on land, and found myself on the Island on Neome, and knowing the country, I perceived I was past Iceland; as the inhabitants were subject to Zichmni* (unknown), *I took in fresh stores, and sailed with a fair wind in three days to Frislanda* (Thorshaven in the Faroes), *where the people, who thought they had lost their prince, in consequence of his long absence on the voyage we had made, received us with a hearty welcome.*

*What happened subsequently to the contents of this letter I* (Nicolo Zeno junior) *gather from conjecture from a piece of another letter, which is to the effect: That Zichmni* (unknown) *settled down in the harbour of his newly discovered island and explored the whole of the country thoroughly as well as the coasts of both sides of Greenland because I find this particular described in the sea charts; but the description is lost.*

It appears that the land just described was not likely Nova Scotia as always believed, but instead Greenland. Yet, the 28 days equals the time needed to sail back to Scotland from Nova Scotia or Newfoundland and not Greenland or Iceland. I am not going to speculate the reasons as for this discrepancy.

The following is a description of Greenland in the 14<sup>th</sup> Century by Ivan Barden: *"It is reported by men of experience, natives of Greenland, and recently come from thence, that from Stad in Norway to Horn on the east coast of Iceland, is seven days sailing due west. From Snaefjeldsnaes in Iceland, from which point the passage to Greenland is the shortest, the course is two days and two nights due west, there you will find Gunnbjorn's Rocks midway between Greenland and Iceland. In old times this was the customary route, but now the ice that had been brought down from the northern...etc.*

*For all the countries round about them are only too glad to traffic* (trade) *with them the two articles just mentioned; and so, without any trouble or expense, they have all that they want. To this monastery Friars resort from Norway, Sweden and other countries, but the greater part come from, the Shetland Islands. A number of vessels are detained continually in the harbor by the frozen sea; they have to wait for the next season and for the ice to melt...Their houses are built about the hill on every side...and the ground below it is so warm that those islands and from the Cape above Norway and from Trondheim* (Treadon). *They bring the Friars all sorts of comforts and take in exchange fish, which they dry in the sun or freeze, and shins of different kinds of animals. So, the Friars obtain wood for burning and admirably carved timber and corn and cloth for clothes...There is a spring of hot water there, which is used to heat both the church of the monastery and the chambers of the Friars...Most of them speak the Latin language, especially the supers and principles of the monastery. This is all that is known of Engroneland* (Greenland) *as described by Sir Nicolo. Who also gives a special description of a river that he discovered, as may be seen in the map that I have drawn. At length, Sir Nicolo, not being used to such severe cold, fell ill. After a while, he returned to Frislanda* (Possibly Fer or Fair Isles, although Frislanda on the Zeno Map refers to the Faroe Islands), *where he died* (Nicolo Zeno died in 1402 back home in Venice.).

*"All these letters were written by Sir Antonio to Sir Carlo, his brother. I am sorry that the book and much else on these subjects have, I don't know, been destroyed. For I was only a child when they fell into my hands, and as I did not know what they were, I tore them in pieces, as children will do, and ruined them. It is something which I cannot now recall without the greatest sorrow. Nevertheless, in order that such an important memoir should be lost, I have put it all in order as well as I could in this narrative. More than its predecessors, the present age may derive pleasure from the great discoveries made in those parts where they were least expected. For our age takes a great interest in new narratives and in the discoveries, made in countries unknown before, by the high courage and great energy of our ancestors."*

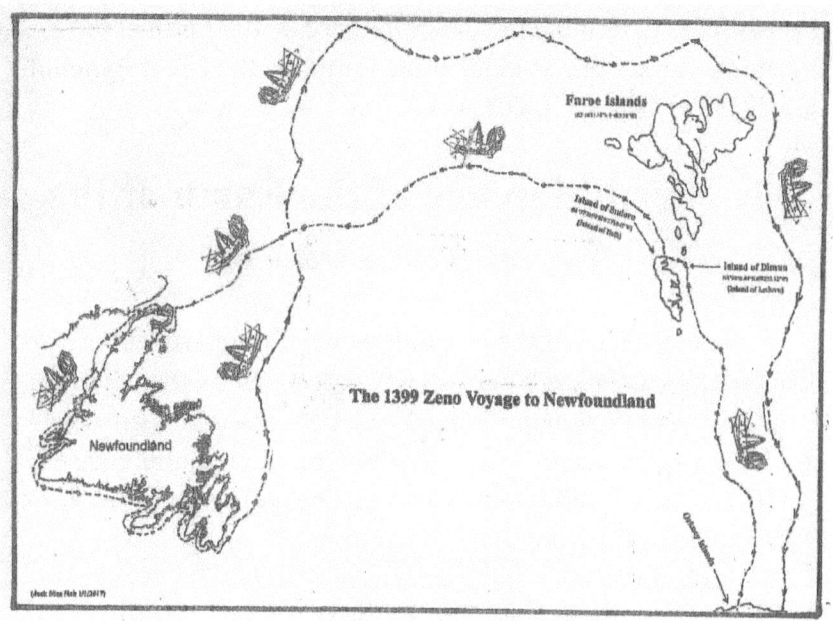

# Chapter 10

# The Atlantis 2-Second Clock

(Invented by Jack Mac Nab in Klagenfurt, Carinthia, Austria, 2019)

In many ways, the Great Pyramid of Giza reminds me of a computer that was assembled like a motherboard with tons and tons of stones. Because of this complexity, I was inspired to invent the Atlantis 2-Second Clock. A couple of key features of this clock are based on the design and construction of the Great Pyramid. It is possible to determine the circumference of the Earth at the Equator and the Polar Radius of the Earth via the Great Pyramid. (GP 29°58'45"N   31°08'03"W)

## 1: Circumference of the Earth at the Equatorial Equator

The distance of the circumference of the Earth at the Equatorial Equator can be accurately calculated by the *"Perimeter of the Base"* of the Great Pyramid of Giza. Based on estimates provided by "Universe Today" the earth has a circumference of 24,901.461 miles. (40,075.017 km) (Space and Astronomy News 2019) (Randall Carlson)

3023.139 ft.   Perimeter of Base of the GP

x482.7575 ft. Height of the GP with the socle

13,0599.604.8 ft. = 24,734.7736 mi. (Circumference of Earth at the Equator via GP)

24,901 mi. (Circumference of the Earth according to Universe Today 2019)

-24,735 mi. (Circumference of Earth at the Equator via the GP)

166 mi. (The GP only fall short by 166 miles of the modern-day calculations)

## 2: Polar Radius of the Earth (North or South Poles)

The distance of the Polar Radius of the Earth from either the North or South Poles can be accurately calculated by multiplying the height of the Great Pyramid, which is 482.7575 feet (including the socle), by the number of seconds to be found in 12 hours, which is 43,200 seconds. According to "Universe Today," to measure from the centre of the Earth to one of the polar-regions, you would obtain a radius of 3,949.9 miles." (Space and Astronomy News 2019, Randall Carlson)

482.7575 ft. = Height of GP (measured with the socle)

x 43.200 sec. = 12 hours

20,855.124 ft. = 3949.834 miles (Polar radius of the Earth)

3949.009 mi.   Radius according to Universe Today 2019

-3949.834 mi. Radius of the Earth via GP height

.066 miles

# The Great Pyramid Represents the Northern-Hemisphere!

The Great Pyramid is a model of One-Hemisphere of the earth at a scale of 1:43,200. The height of the Great Pyramid (482.7575 ft.) measured with the *Socle* is 1/43,200th part of the Earth's polar radius. (Socle 3043.433 ft.) (Randall Carlson)

## Equator and ½ Second of Time

In ½ second of time at a point on the equator will rotate a distance equal to one-side of the base, of the Great Pyramid measured with the Socle." (½ second time is 1/172, 800th part of the Diurnal Rotation., Randall Carlson)

## Equator: 2 Seconds of Time

Given 2 seconds of Time (1/43,200th part of the Diurnal rotation) a point on the equator will travel a distance precisely equal to the perimeter of the Great Pyramid Base measured with the Socle. (Pyramid Socle: 21.65 inches thick with a perimeter of 3043.433 feet) (Randel Carlson)

Perimeter of the GP at the Base  = 3023.139 ft.

Perimeter of the GP at the Socle = 3043.433 ft.

## Perimeter GP at the Base: 3023.139 ft.

North 755.421 ft.

South 756.081 ft.

East 755.874 ft.

West 755.763 ft.

## Perimeter GP at the Socle: 3043.433 ft.

North 760.817 ft.

South 760.783 ft.

East 759.933 ft.

West 760.900 ft.

## Speed of Light

The location of the Great Pyramid appears to have been determined by its distance from the equator. When the latitude number is matched with the speed of light, these numbers then become very interesting!

29.9792 458°N  - Latitude of GP

299.792.458 m/s - Speed of Light

I am inclined to believe that the moving of the decimal point was of interest to people of ancient times as well! This moving of the decimal point proves to reveal some mathematics that may only appear to some people as being coincidental. Take, for example, the 23,200 seconds in one half day! (12 hours) Divide

23,200 by 3 =14.400. Move the decimal one unit to the right and we have 144.000.

3 – 23,200 = 14.400 (Move decimal point = 144.000)

2 – 144 = 72.00 (Remove the decimal point = 72 and the 000)

Where is this leading? It confirms to me why various groups of people used these numbers 144 and 72 to solve some mathematical mysteries of our sun, moon and planets.

## Diameter-&-Radius of the Sun-&-Moon via Time

864.400 mi. = Diameter Sun

86.400 sec. = 24 hours

432.000 mi. = Radius of Sun

43.200 sec. = 12 hours

2.160 mi. = Diameter of Moon

21.600 sec. = 6 hours

1080 mi. = Radius of Moon

10.800 sec. = 3 hours

# The following numbers may come in handy some day!

7917 mi  = Diameter of Earth

3950 mi  = Radius of Earth

## The Randall Carlson YouTube Videos:

The mathematical formula for "The Atlantis 2 Second Clock" has been accurately calculated by mathematician Randall Carlson. Carlson's YouTube Videos:

Randall Carlson – The Great Pyramid Part 1

Randall Carlson – The Great Pyramid Part 2

Randall Carlson – The Great Pyramid Part 3

## The Jack Mac Nab YouTube Videos:

The Great Pyramid 2 Second Clock = Oak Island Nova Scotia (Part 1)

The Great Pyramid 2 Second Clock = Great Pyramid of Giza (Part 2)

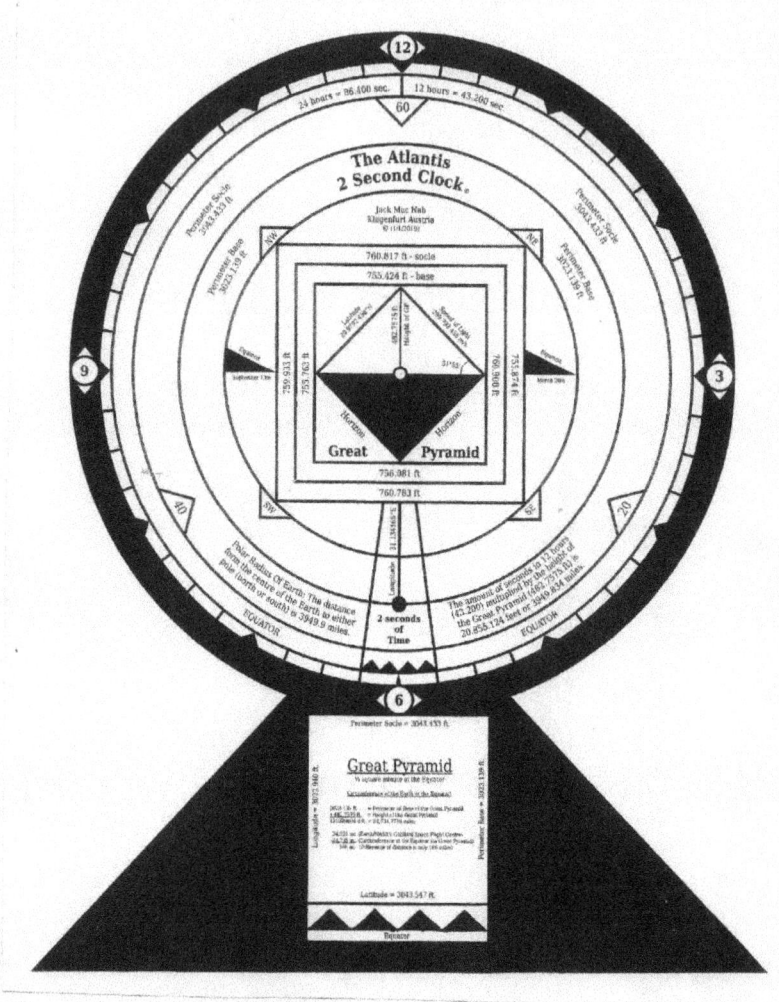

# Chapter 11

## Oak Island and the Azimuth Lines

(Oak Island Nova Scotia 44°30'54.70" N 64°17'32.05"W)

  As mentioned earlier, there are two large and two small drumlins located on Oak Island. Drumlins are elongated, oval shaped hills made up of various layers of bedrock, mainly of the type known as Ordovician Halifax-formation slate. It is claimed that about 8-10,000 years ago that Oak Island was part of a large *lagoon* that encompassed most of the Mahone Bay area. At that time Oak Island was *not an island* but was instead connected to the mainland. There is no doubt in my mind that the Old Gold River made its way through this *lagoon* near the location of present-day Oak Island. The old *river bed* is clearly spotted on the bottom of that bay by means of side-scan-sonar equipment. (Oak Island: 44°30'54.70"N 64°17'32.05"W)

  Over the years, I have discovered that several azimuth lines cross over that pinhead landmass know today as Oak Island. All these azimuth lines begin at *key* locations, end at key locations on planet earth, and cross directly over Oak Island. How could this be possible? Is this only a coincidence? Time will tell.

  According to Wikipedia: "An azimuth is an angular measurement in a spherical coordinate system. The vector from an observer (origin) to a point of interest is projected perpendicularly onto a reference plane; the angle between the projected vector and a reference vector on the reference plane is called the azimuth.

"When used as a celestial coordinate, the azimuth is the horizontal direction of a star or other astronomical object in the sky. The star is the point of interest and the reference plane is the local area around an observer on Earth's surface, and the reference vector points to true north. The azimuth is the angle between the north vector and the star's vector on the horizontal plane.

"Today, the reference plane for an azimuth is typically true north, measured as a 0° azimuth, though other angular units (grad, mil) can be used. Moving clockwise on a 360 degree-circle and east has azimuth 90°, south 180°, and west 270°. There are exceptions: some navigation systems use south as the reference vector. Any direction can be the reference vector, as long as it is clearly defined."

## The Great Pyramid Giza

It is very plausible that when constructing the Great Pyramid of Giza (2580 - 2560 BC), the designers were no doubt as mush aware of azimuths lines as they were with latitude and longitude lines.

To explain my theory, one can only assume what might have taken place based on a few *facts*. For example, I have discovered an azimuth line begins at the Great Pyramid of Giza and ends at the Washington D.C. Temple in Kensington, Maryland, Washington D.C. There was no known Temple on that location when that construction project began. This is a distance of 5,800 miles (9,400 km). How could an azimuth line this long be made possible? I will attempt to explain my hypothesis!

Great Pyramid on the Giza Plateau:   29°0'58.45"N 31°O8'45"E

Washington D.C. Temple, Maryland: 39°0'50.70"N - 77°3'56.42"W

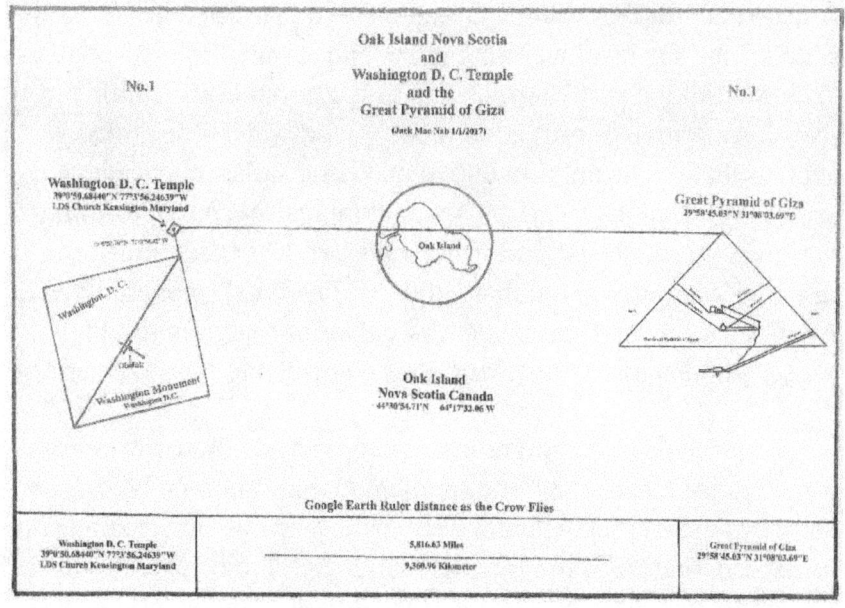

Creating azimuth lines for short distance travel when on a ship is old news. To sail across the Atlantic Ocean in ancient times and create an azimuth line 3-5000 miles long is another issue! A straight line as the crow flies could only be created after reaching that desired location.

According to Plato, the Egyptian high priest revealed to Solon the general location of the Island of Atlantis,"which was…*outside the Pillars of Heracles*…an island greater in extent than Libya and Asia, and afterwards *sunk* by an earthquake, became an ***impassible barrier of mud*** to voyagers sailing from hence to any part of the oceans…during all this time through changes…the earth has fallen away all round and sunk out of sight (Island of Atlantis sunk to the bottom of the Atlantic Ocean)…the consequences in comparison of what then was, there are remaining only the ***bones of the wasted body***, as they are called, as in the case of ***small islands***, all the richer and softer parts of the soil having fallen away, and a mere ***skeleton of land being left***."

**Author:** As for the Atlantic Ocean prior to that "Deluge of flood-waters," the sea level was a lot lower and it was peppered with *"islands"* all the way to the shores of the "Boundless Continent" (North America). Shortly after those "flood-waters" subsided, it appears that it was not possible to make transatlantic voyages across the Atlantic Ocean due to that *"impassable barrier of mud."* Following those Post-flood-water days, sea levels continued to rise, and it appears to me that 1000's of *"islands"* peppered the Atlantic Ocean, and this made it possible for seafarers to sail across all the way to the *"Boundless Continent,"* North America.

It seems that a migration of people made their way across the Atlantic Oceans via these small and large *"islands."* No doubt these voyages on the Atlantic were made possible by the small and large reed-boats. For the Egyptian High Priest to be able to inform Solon that there was a *"Boundless Continent"* on the opposite side of the Atlantic Ocean, someone would have had to have made a voyage to the shores of the Americas, and returned to Egypt with this information.

This would logically support the theory that has been debated for many years, that there were, in ancient times, trade routes established between the Old World and the New World. As the centuries passed, these trade routes started to fall out of use, when many of these *"islands"* became submerged due to the rising sea level. These islands today are referred to as Phantom Islands.

By means of reed-boats, mariners would zigzag from island-to-island as they made their voyage across the Atlantic Ocean. On or near any of these *"islands,"* it was possible to take coordinates readings needed for a return voyage. It is my belief that those ancient seafarers were well aware of the size of the equatorial circumference and the polar-radius of earth. Their having a very accurate knowledge of the latitude and longitude lines was a given based on my findings.

Once on the soil of North America, coordinate readings would be taken and possibly marked down on a papyrus map, along with all the *"islands"* where coordinates were taken. Once back in Egypt, this zigzag *"islands"* coordinates would be made straight. Hence, an azimuth line has been created. This and other azimuth lines would be used for future trade routes. That azimuth line would be as straight as the crow flies. This would be an invisible azimuth line to the naked eye, in the same manner as invisible latitude and longitude lines are to this very day. Yet, on globe maps they are visible lines, as we see them today on any modern map.

When I refer to drawing azimuth lines on maps, these maps in ancient times would be in the shape of an earth-globe! Azimuth lines do not work on flat surface maps. Globes make it possible to include the curvature of the earth when using azimuth lines.

Then the sun would be used as good a reference point as any star when determining an azimuth line. Without instruments, an azimuth line can be created and accurately determined by tracing a simple cross in the sand on any beach. The same applies when on a ship with a few sticks, etc.

## **America's Stonehenge**

Another site of interest is what is known America's Stonehenge, located in the general area of Salem, New Hampshire, U.S.A. It was formerly known as Mystery Hill for many years. Some claim that the site was constructed at least 4,000 years ago. It appears that people in the so-called "professional world" appear to believe that it was constructed by a farmer in the 1800's.

I am personally inclined to believe that it is an ancient site. But I have no way of proving that view to be a *fact*. What I do find interesting is that an azimuth line begins at America's Stonehenge and crosses over pinhead Oak Island, crosses the Atlantic Ocean and hits North Africa. Then I cherry picked a location that I felt had a good potential of where it should end.

That specific location is Cape Matifou, Algeria. It is shaped like a finger, as if pointing to the *"Boundless Continent,"* better known as North America.

America's Stonehenge: 42°50'31.67" N 71°12'35.10"W

Cape Matifou Algeria: 36°48'44.34"N 3°13'24.19"E

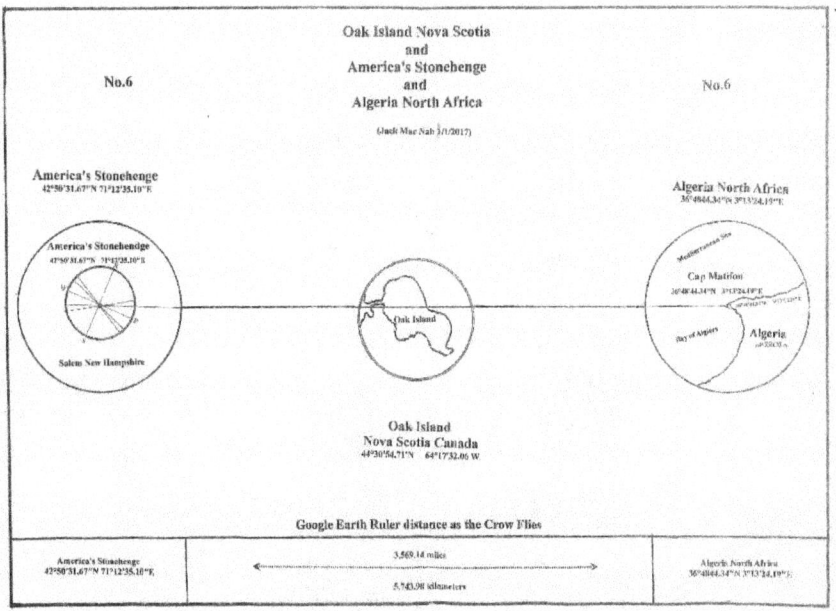

So, I am just presenting this claim as being very *plausible*. What I like about that general location is that, in ancient times, it was known a Numidia. There are two theories in this book that have connections to ancient Numidia and ancient Mauretania.

No.1: Queen Scotia Voyage (Late 14th Century B.C.)

No.2: Alexander Helios Voyage (Late 1st Century A.D)

Once again, Berber (Tifinagh) characters are carved on the HO-stone on Oak Island, and now a connection with the Berbers of North Africa via America's Stonehenge. For all I know maybe America's Stonehenge was constructed in Atlantis prior to the destruction via the Plato's "Deluge of flood-waters." Just another mystery to think about, etc.

## Cleopatra's Hieroglyphics

Now connect an azimuth line with the Cleopatra's Hieroglyphics located in at Admiral's Cove in Bedford Basin, Nova Scotia, then cross that line over Oak Island. Where it ends may just be a coincidence! It ends at the Cleopatra Needle located in Central Park, New York, New York.

Cleopatra's Hieroglyphics Admiral's Cove Bedford NS:
44°42'56.61"N - 63°39'24.72"W

Cleopatra's Needle (Obelisk) Central Park New York City:
40°46'46.51" - N 73°57'53.36"W

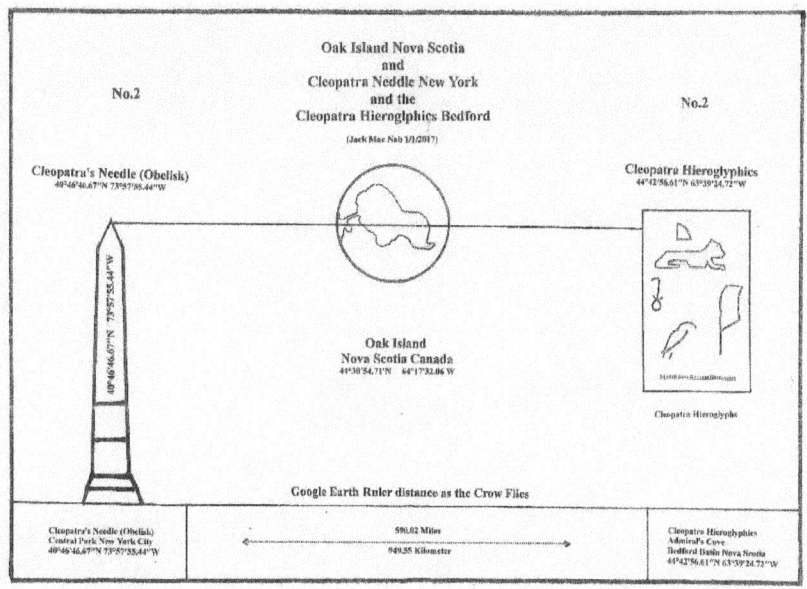

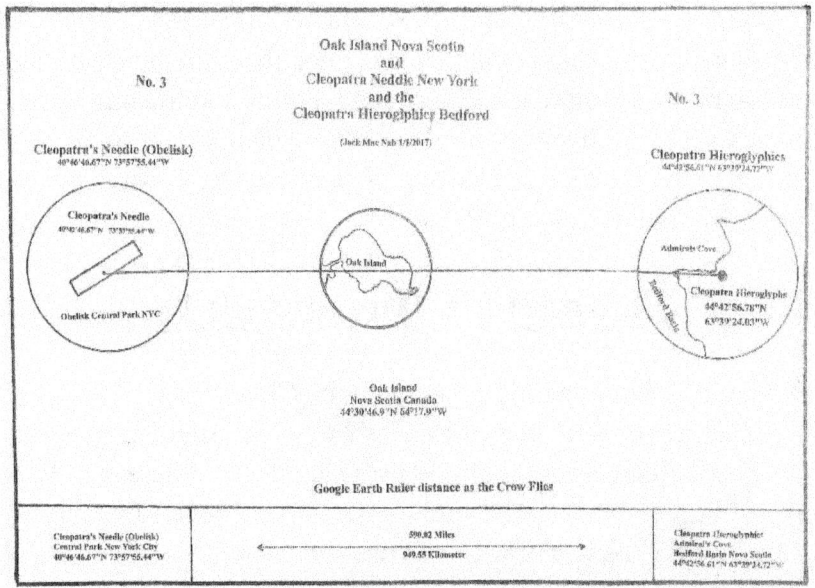

# Washington Monument

I am inclined to believe that, in *fact,* an azimuth line that is connected to the Egyptian Obelisk located in St. Peter's Square crosses over Oak Island, and ends at the Washington Monument in Washington D.C.

Washington Monument (Obelisk) Washington D.C: 38°53'22.05"N - 77°2'4.80"W

St. Peter's Square (Obelisk) Vatican City Rome: 41°54'8.1"N - 12°27'26.1"

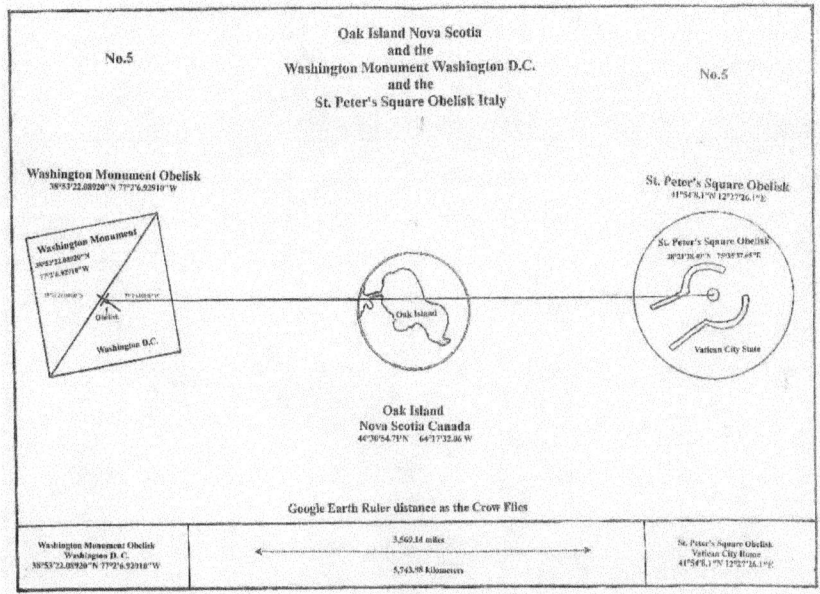

This subject of the azimuth line is to be viewed as an ongoing investigation on my part. Who may have known about these azimuth lines is still an unsolved mystery at this point in time, although I suspect that secret societies in the Old World and the New World before and after 1492 may have known of their existence. You will certainly hear more from me on this issue in a possible future follow-up book. Thanks for reading.

## International Azimuth Lines
(Jack Mac Nab 1/1/2017)

No.3 azimuth reading is not included on this chart. There is another chart where it is located for other purposes related to this chart. On this chart to the far right it is listed as "A" under the title The Eight Egyptian Obelisk of Rome. "A" reads: Piazza di Giovanni in (Laterano) Tuthmosis III/Tuthmosis IV.

**Google Earth Ruler distance as the Crow Flies**

| | | | | |
|---|---|---|---|---|
| Washington D. C. Temple 39°0'56.6840"N 75°3'56.2463"W LDS Church Kensington Maryland | No.1 | ← 5,816.63 Miles → <br> 9,360.96 Kilometer | No.1 | Great Pyramid of Giza 29°58'45.03"N 31°08'03.09"E |
| Cleopatra's Needle (Obelisk) Central Park New York City 40°46'46.67"N 73°57'58.44"W | No.2 | ← 590.02 Miles → <br> 949.55 Kilometer | No.2 | Cleopatra Hieroglyphics Admiral's Cove Bedford Basin Nova Scotia 44°41'56.61"N 63°39'24.72"W |
| Washington Monument Obelisk Washington D. C. 38°53'22.00930"N 77°2'6.92910"W | No.5 | ← 3,569.14 miles → <br> 5,743.98 kilometers | No.5 | St. Peter's Square Obelisk Vatican City Rome 41°54'8.3"N 12°27'26.1"E |
| America's Stonehenge 42°50'31.67"N 71°12'35.10"E | No.6 | ← 3,569.14 miles → <br> 5,743.98 kilometers | No.6 | Cape Masifou Algeria North Africa 36°48'44.34"N 3°13'24.19"E |
| Salisbury Maryland United States 38°21'38.49"N 75°38'57.65"W | No.7 | ← 3,569.14 miles → <br> 5,743.98 kilometers | No.7 | Stonehenge England Wiltshire England 51°10'43.84"N 1°49'34.10"W |
| Temple of Umgiebems Penobscot Maine 44°30'54.73"N 68°48'0.94"W | No.8 | 2,725.43 Miles <br> 4,386.15 Kilometer | Oak Island Nova Scotia Canada 44°30'54.71"N 64°17'32.06 W | |

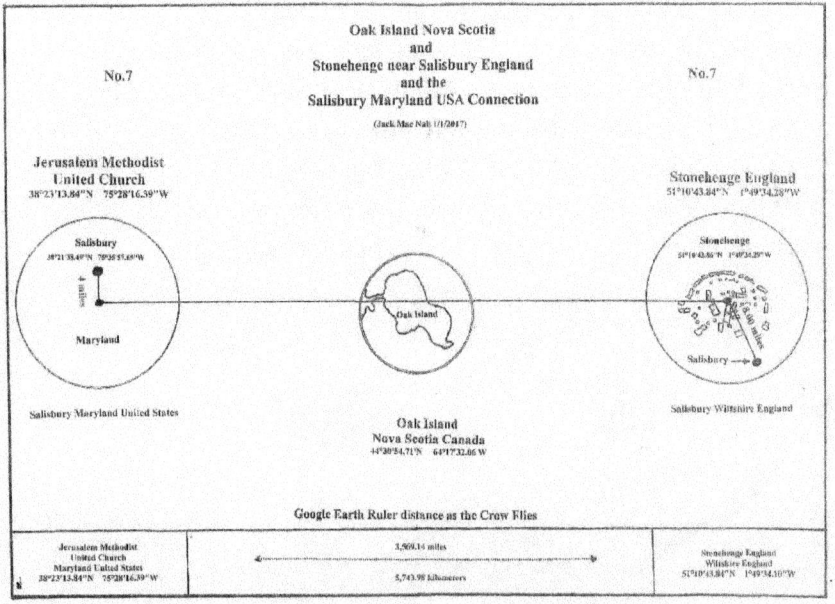

Oak Island Nova Scotia
and
Stonehenge near Salisbury England
and the
Salisbury Maryland USA Connection
(Jack Mac Nab 1/1/2017)

No.7 — No.7

Jerusalem Methodist United Church 38°23'13.84"N 75°28'16.39"W

Stonehenge England 51°10'43.84"N 1°49'34.28"W

Salisbury Maryland United States

Oak Island Nova Scotia Canada 44°30'54.71'N 64°17'32.06 W

Salisbury Wiltshire England

**Google Earth Ruler distance as the Crow Flies**

| | | |
|---|---|---|
| Jerusalem Methodist United Church Maryland United States 38°23'13.84"N 75°28'16.39"W | ← 3,569.14 miles → <br> 5,743.98 kilometers | Stonehenge England Wiltshire England 51°10'43.84"N 1°49'34.10"W |

114

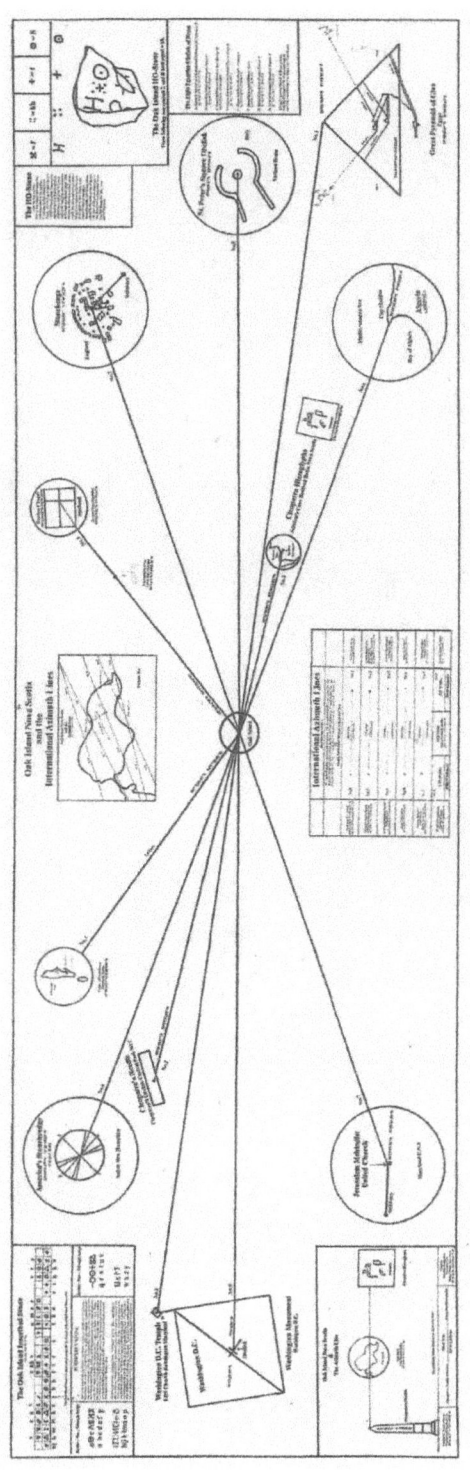

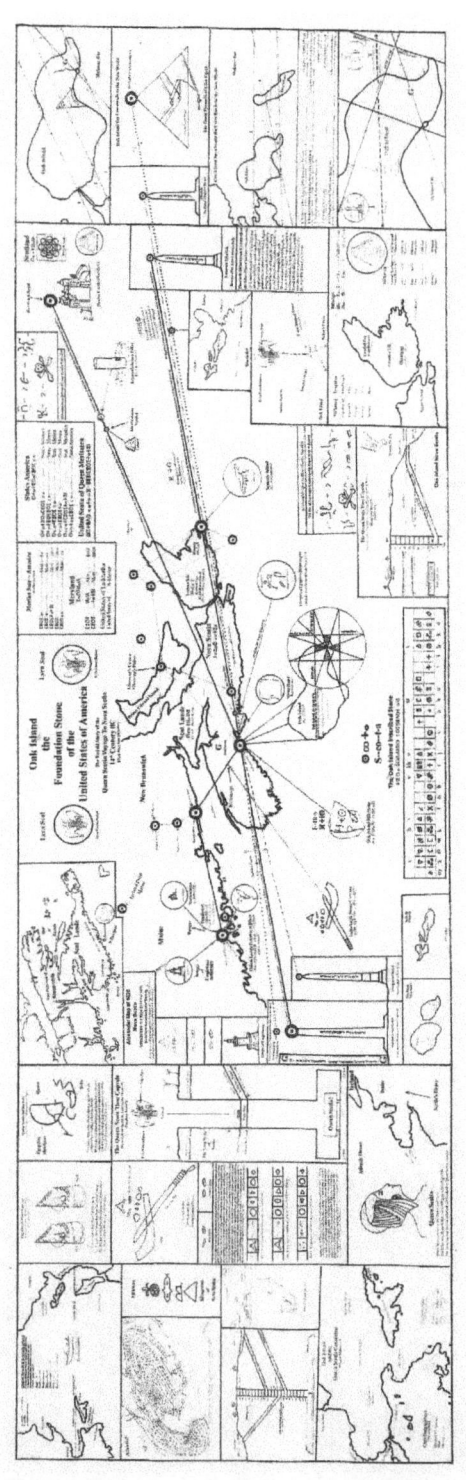

www.ingramcontent.com/pod-product-compliance
Lightning Source LLC
LaVergne TN
LVHW011210080426
835508LV00007B/704